# Steps into God's Grace

*Spiritual Formation through God's Word and the 12 Steps of Recovery*

Lynn Hoffmann

© Copyright 2013

All rights reserved

ISBN-13: 978-1490451114 (CreateSpace-Assigned)

ISB -10: 1490451110

Scripture quotations identified by:

- AMP are taken from the *Amplified Bible*, Copyright © 1954, 1958, 1962, 1964, 1965, 1987 by The Lockman Foundation. Used by permission. (www.Lockman.org)
- MSG are taken from *The Message*, Copyright © 1993, 1994, 1995, 1996, 2000, 2001, 2002. Used by permission of NavPress Publishing Group.
- NASB are from the *New American Standard Bible®*, Copyright © 1960, 1962, 1963, 1968, 1971, 1972, 1973, 1975, 1977, 1995 by The Lockman Foundation, Used by permission. (www.Lockman.org)
- NLT are taken from the *Holy Bible*, New Living Translation, copyright 1996, 2004, 2007 by Tyndale House Foundation. Used by permission of Tyndale House Publishers, Inc., Carol Stream, Illinois 60188. All rights reserved.

# DEDICATION

To my dear husband Dick Hoffmann, without your encouragement this study might never have been written. Through your challenging questions and edits, you provided clarity and insight that was greatly needed.

To Jan Winebrenner, my faithful friend, for your tireless, professional guidance which made each word on the page communicate my mission and God's Truth.

To the ladies in my Tuesday group, for participating in this study over many weeks, months and years, and praying for me as I waited for God to reveal His Truth.

Many thanks to each of you for sharing my vision to see people come to know God intimately, be transformed by His grace and live an abundant life with Him today!

# AUTHOR

Lynn Hoffmann was born and raised in rural Rhode Island and later moved to southern Florida. She ultimately graduated from The University of Texas at Dallas with a degree in accounting. She raised three children and founded a regional commercial real estate company in which she served as the President.

After a failed first marriage, God called Lynn into a deep personal relationship with Jesus. As Lynn grew spiritually, she continued to struggle with the realities of life that were brought on with work, a new husband and blending a family.

During these struggles, God graciously led Lynn into a 12 Step recovery group that provided a foundation for her personal healing and transformation.

Lynn mentors women, teaches Bible studies and loves to read and be by the water. She and her husband of 18 years live in Dallas, Texas.

Lynn can be contacted at lynn@stepsintogodsgrace.com.

# STEPS INTO GOD'S GRACE

## Table of Contents

| | | |
|---|---|---|
| Forward……………………………………………………………… | | i |
| Introduction………………………………………………………… | | ii |
| My Story……………………………………………………………… | | iii |

### PART ONE: THE TRUTH GOD WANTS ME TO KNOW

| | | | |
|---|---|---|---|
| Lesson 1 | | The Journey………………………………………… | 2 |
| Lesson 2 | Step 1 | Who Am I?…………………………………………… | 9 |
| Lesson 3 | Step 1 | What is Wrong?…………………………………… | 16 |
| Lesson 4 | Step 2 | Where is Our Hope?……………………………… | 23 |
| Lesson 5 | Step 2 | God's Rescue Plan………………………………… | 28 |
| Lesson 6 | Step 2 | Do You Believe?…………………………………… | 34 |
| Lesson 7 | Step 3 | King of My Kingdom……………………………… | 40 |
| Lesson 8 | Step 3 | Will You Rebel or Surrender?………………… | 45 |
| Lesson 9 | Step 3 | Receive New Life in God's Kingdom………… | 51 |

### PART TWO: THE WAY GOD WANTS TO TRANSFORM ME

| | | | |
|---|---|---|---|
| Lesson 10 | Step 3 | Led into the Way………………………………… | 59 |
| Lesson 11 | Step 4 | The Oasis of Examination……………………… | 65 |
| Lesson 12 | Step 4 | At the Oasis: Inventory-Part One…………… | 72 |
| Lesson 13 | Step 4 | At the Oasis: Inventory-Part Two…………… | 80 |
| Lesson 14 | Step 4 | Blessing at the Oasis…………………………… | 87 |
| Lesson 15 | Step 5 | The Mountain of Confession-Part One……… | 92 |
| Lesson 16 | Step 5 | The Mountain of Confession-Part Two……… | 97 |
| Lesson 17 | Step 6 | The Valley of Repentance……………………… | 104 |
| Lesson 18 | Step 7 | The Pool of Transformation…………………… | 112 |
| Lesson 19 | Step 8 | The River of Forgiveness……………………… | 116 |
| Lesson 20 | Step 9 | The Pathway to Peace-Part One……………… | 121 |
| Lesson 21 | Step 9 | The Pathway to Peace-Part Two……………… | 125 |

### PART THREE: THE LIFE GOD WANTS ME TO ENJOY

| | | | |
|---|---|---|---|
| Lesson 22 | Step 10 | Hold Fast to the Truth and the Way………… | 132 |
| Lesson 23 | Step 11 | Be Rooted in God's Love……………………… | 139 |
| Lesson 24 | Step 11 | Love God …………………………………………… | 145 |
| Lesson 25 | Step 12 | Love Yourself……………………………………… | 150 |
| Lesson 26 | Step 12 | Love Others ……………………………………… | 159 |
| Lesson 27 | Step 12 | You are the Message of God's Love………… | 169 |

### APPENDICIES

| | |
|---|---|
| The Twelve Steps………………………………………………………… | A-1 |
| Optional Readings……………………………………………………… | A-2 |

# Forward

I had coffee with Lynn for the first time ten years ago. I remember it like it was yesterday. I talked. She listened. She didn't say more than a few words, but when I had drained my cup and it was time to leave, I was already trying to figure out when we could get together again. A week later she agreed to meet again. And the next week. And the next. Now, ten years later, we still meet weekly, sometimes more. Lynn is still the same woman I was drawn to all those years ago. She is full of confidence in Jesus, assured of His love for her and quick to share that truth. She is calm, soft-spoken, gentle and wise. Nothing different there. But I am different. Because Lynn listened to me like no one ever had. She honored my story with probing questions, seeking to hear not only my words but also my heart. And in doing so, she gave me room to grow and become a different person, one who is braver than she used to be, one who is growing more peaceful, more trusting, more quiet, and more in love with Jesus than ever imagined. One who has begun to enjoy the walk of faith after decades of struggle and disappointment.

Lynn introduced me to the 12 Steps.

She shared my Recovery journey, coming alongside me, always pointing me to Jesus, while introducing me to principles and ways of doing life and relationships that revolutionized my ideas of God's love for me, His purpose for me and His ways of living the life of faith.

Not everyone is so fortunate as to be able to spend time with Lynn over a coffee cup every week, but now, because of *Steps Into God's Grace,* anyone can join her, and countless other Christians who have discovered the Christ-based 12 Steps to be the discipleship model we have desperately needed, a model for the life God calls us to—a life of desperate dependence on Jesus that leads to unexpected joy.

I just wish they could all have coffee with Lynn.

*Jan Winebrenner* ~ Author
*Intimate Faith,* Warner
*The Grace of Catastrophe,* Moody

# STEPS INTO GOD'S GRACE

# Introduction

Are you confused, afraid or suffering? Do you feel burdened by guilt or shame over past or present failures? Do you struggle with painful life circumstances that you feel powerless to control? Do you wonder where God is and why He doesn't seem to help? Do you feel confused about the promise of abundant life and wonder why you're missing out?

You are not alone. I began life with many hopes and dreams, yet over time I felt beaten and battered by life circumstances or my poor choices. Confused and overwhelmed, I forced myself to conform my *outside* to what was expected of me by trying to achieve greater accomplishments, acquire more things and perfect my image. Yet *inside*, despite all this effort, I was filled with sadness, emptiness, insecurity and loneliness. So began my quest to find hope and peace in my life.

Trusting in Jesus Christ as my Lord and Savior, studying the Bible, participating in 12 Step recovery programs and learning to listen and respond to the loving wisdom of the Holy Spirit caused significant changes in my life. I have personally experienced God's healing from shame and guilt of my past and freedom from the need for approval from others. Now that I live with a desperate dependence on God alone, I have peace I never had before.

The journey was not easy. I encountered, and continue to encounter, many obstacles. But daily God convinces me that He is my only hope.

That is why I'm inviting you to join me and enter into a similar transformational, discipleship journey with God. On this journey we will not just be students who learn more information, but disciples who, empowered by the Holy Spirit, learn the Truth, the Way and the Life. On the journey we will have our thinking challenged, our understanding expanded, our hearts opened and our wounds healed. We will become participants, not spectators, in God's plan and purpose.

My prayer for you is that along the way, God will help you recover the truth of who you really are and who He is. I pray also that you will grow in your trust of Him as you come to know His goodness and unfailing love for you.

As we take this journey together, I pray you will mysteriously and miraculously experience the healing power of God in your life. I pray you will enter into a love relationship with Him that is more amazing than you ever imagined or hoped for as He redeems, heals and restores you to your true identity and inheritance as His child living in His Kingdom of Grace.

# **MY STORY**

Before I began walking with God and experiencing healing, I felt like a puppet. Behind my painted face and dressed up body was a silent, unreal person struggling to be loved for who she really was. I know now that I was controlled by so many fears and expectations that I couldn't be real. Even more, I couldn't stop responding whenever someone pulled one of my strings, demanding me to be who they wanted me to be. These strings, and the people pulling them, controlled my life.

Exhausted from resisting, I gave up trying to be me. Silently, I acquiesced to the puppeteers in my life and let them have control of the strings—strings I came to recognize as fear of abandonment, fear of rejection, fear of failure, and fear of not being enough; strings that, when yanked, sent me into activity, hoping to somehow escape the feelings of guilt and shame, and the fear of being a disappointment. I accepted that it was best for me to just be whatever or whoever others expected me to be. I tried through my performance and my caretaking to please them so I could be happy. After years of attempting to live life this way, however, I found myself sobbing on my bed, my life in broken pieces. In the middle of a divorce, desperate for help, I cried out to God to rescue me. A family member soon led me to Christ. Mercifully, God directed me to a church and gently began to teach me truth.

A few years after I became a believer, I entered a very difficult time in my second marriage. I began to question my faith. All my efforts to read my bible, attend church, and serve God were not gaining my desired results for a better life. What was wrong? I still felt desperate, lost, empty and alone much of the time. I was exhausted from trying to be good! My eyes were swollen from crying. I failed to see any answers to my fearful prayers for help! *There has to be more to a spiritual life than this,* I thought.

When a friend suggested I consider a 12 Step Recovery program, I was willing (even though I was not an alcoholic). I was desperate. Nothing else was working for me. And it was through that program that the Holy Spirit and the Word of God began to teach me the truth about who I am: I am *not* a puppet; I *am* a human being who is greatly loved by her Heavenly Father. Gently, but with determination, God took my hand and led me, sometimes kicking and screaming, showing me how to let go of old burdens. One by one he freed me from my puppet strings. He began to heal my broken heart. He helped me forgive. Along the way my heart grew full of love for Him. He was becoming more fully God to me, and I was becoming more of the human He created me to be.

I now know that, from the time I was first baptized as a child and christened with the name Ann, meaning "full of grace", God has been lovingly teaching me and preparing me to share His love and grace. Out of my journey, He has prompted me to write this study, <u>Steps into God's Grace.</u>

# STEPS INTO GOD'S GRACE

## PART ONE: THE TRUTH GOD WANTS ME TO KNOW

> *We must see the soul and the person in its ruined condition, with its malformed and dysfunctional mind, feelings, body, and social relations, before we can understand that it must be delivered and reformed and how that can be done. One of the greatest obstacles to effective spiritual formation in Christ today is simple failure to understand and acknowledge the reality of the human situation as it affects Christians and non-Christians alike. We must start from where we really are.* (*Renovation of the Heart* by Dallas Willard, p. 45)

# STEPS INTO GOD'S GRACE

## LESSON 1: The Journey

*"Your life is a journey you must travel with a deep consciousness of God."* (1 Peter 1:18 MSG)

## THE JOURNEY

This study calls us to take a journey which will bring us into a new spiritual awakening about ourselves, God and others. If we bring a willing heart and an open mind, we will come to know the truth of who we are and who God is. Then, in the reality of these truths, we will each be challenged to consider how we should live.

As we begin this journey together, each of us comes as a child seeking healing, seeking wholeness, wisdom, and God. Many of us desire to know the truth and are looking for freedom from our pain and confusion. This is not a journey we can take alone. Although we will have to do our own work by reading scripture, reflecting on questions, considering circumstances in our own lives, coming to meetings, and sharing as honestly as we can, we will find that much of our learning also comes from listening to what others share about themselves and what God is doing in their lives.

Our guide is the Holy Spirit who we will trust to show us the way. We will have to stay close to Him to learn His voice and follow when He calls so we will not wander away.

Each of us will bring bags full of our treasures–our past, our friends and families, and our valuable things. What is in our bags may be different, but our destination is the same.

As we walk along with each other, we will be fed new food; much of it will be different from anything we have had before. We will be asked to look at things we would rather not look at and hear things we would rather not hear. We will be taught new ways to live.

Sometimes we will stop and unpack our bags. We may decide some items are no longer necessary or too heavy to carry any further. We may choose to leave some of them behind in order to move ahead.

Along the way, we will depend upon each other for encouragement and strength.

Little by little, with each new step, we will come to realize that we are changing. Our minds are becoming renewed and our hearts are being healed. Little by little, the fears that have controlled us are diminishing and the unforgiveness that has caused us such pain and agony is gone.

And one day, we will look back at all the valleys, mountains, deserts, and rivers we crossed and realize it was all worth it. While we were looking at the difficulties and impossible situations, God was very lovingly and carefully restoring us to our true identity and inheritance in the midst of them. He was carrying out His promise to us to never leave us or forsake us. He was carrying out His promise to complete the work He began. He was recovering and restoring us to new life and equipping us to live as His beloved children in His Kingdom of Grace.

***As you reflect on this description of the journey you are about to enter, what do you find most encouraging?***
_____
_____

***discouraging?***_____
_____
_____

***Are you ready to go on such a journey?*** _____

## THE STUDY

This study is composed of weekly lessons which encompass the following:

<u>The Word</u>: We will study the Holy Bible to know the truth of who we are, who God is and how we should then live. Scripture references will come from various versions, including The Message, which is a paraphrase, not a direct translation. *"If you abide in My word (hold fast to my teachings and live in accordance with them), you are truly my disciples."* <u>John 8:31 (AMP)</u>

<u>The Holy Spirit</u>: Relying on the Holy Spirit, we will be guided into understanding of God's truth, transformed by the truth and empowered to walk in that truth. *"All who are led by the Spirit of God are sons of God."* <u>Romans 8:14 (AMP)</u>

<u>The 12 Steps of Alcoholics Anonymous</u>: This series of 12 steps, developed by people who were desperate to recover from addiction, are biblical and life changing. While we may not be seeking to recover from addiction, these steps work for any of us who are seeking to mature spiritually. The practice of these spiritual steps, some of which include examination, confession, repentance, and forgiveness, allow us to come to know more of God's truth and His love for us and enable us to experience His power and presence in our life. We will recover who God created us to be and experience restoration of our relationship with God, self and others.

<u>Readings and Questions</u>: Each lesson is structured to include scripture and principles from one of the 12 Steps. You will be asked to complete one lesson per week with questions that challenge your mind, heart and actions. It is very important that you take the time to consider each of the questions, complete them honestly and participate in the group discussions.

<u>Step into God's Grace</u>: Everything from God is grace--unmerited favor toward each of us who believe. It comes in many forms, including revelation, salvation, forgiveness,

redemption, restoration, healing and relationship. Grace has always been available, but we seldom apprehend it fully. As we proceed on our journey, with each step we take, a door is opened for us to receive more of God's grace.

Small group time: It is not safe or wise to go on an unknown journey by ourselves. We need companions who encourage and support us along the way. We do that by regularly attending meetings and participating in the discussion of the key points of each lesson.

Prayer: It is important that we commit to pray for each other during the week as we seek to strengthen each other on this journey.

Mentor/Sponsor: In addition to the Holy Spirit and the group, we each need someone to walk with us who has taken this journey previously. It is recommended that you choose someone you trust and are willing to welcome into all areas of your life. You commit to faithfully meet often with this person to honestly discuss your specific struggles and progress through the steps.

## **SAFE PLACE**

While we are coming to know each other as companions on this journey we will seek to create a room of truth, grace, forgiveness and confidentiality in our small group time. Our desire is for this to be a place where we all can be authentic and share honestly with each other our doubts, fears and failures. We can also acknowledge how we see God working in the midst of our life circumstances. The following guidelines are necessary for this to be a safe place.

1. We will listen attentively and respectfully to what is shared without passing judgment.

2. We will seek to encourage and support each other and not attempt to fix or change one another.

3. We will not repeat what is shared in the group.

***Do you agree to honor the guidelines of the group?* _____**

***What will be the most challenging guideline for you--attentively listening, not offering advice or keeping a confidence?***
_____

Having a safe place will provide opportunities for authenticity, learning and growth.

***How would you present yourself differently if you believed this was a safe place?***
_____
_____

## SHARING

We implement the above guidelines to create a safe place to facilitate sharing honestly. Vulnerable honesty may be difficult at first. For me, I knew how to talk about everyone else and their problems, but I had long ago denied or ignored my own struggles, thoughts and feelings. Sometimes, I was so focused on trying to be who others expected me to be, or who I thought I should be, I didn't know what my real thoughts and feelings were. Sometimes I was unwilling to be honest because I was afraid of what others would think of me or that they might criticize me. Yet this isolated me from myself and others. When I pretended to be who I imagined I should be, hiding my true thoughts and feelings, I was not honest, authentic or real.

Being in a safe place with others who are sharing honestly helps us reconnect with our own hidden or deep doubts, wounds or struggles. Hearing others sharing many of the same thoughts and feelings helps us know we are not alone.

You are encouraged to verbalize your questions and struggles with your life, the lesson, or God's ways during our meeting time. Your words, however, should be focused only on your own thoughts, feelings and behaviors, not those of another.

*Are you more comfortable talking about your thoughts, feelings and behaviors or those of someone else? Why?*

---

## FEELINGS

In the past, all I could say was I felt overwhelmed and tired most of the time. A counselor once told me that I was very intuitive about was going on with others but did not have a clue about what was going on with me. I have come to understand that I was so focused on what everyone else felt or needed that I had denied or ignored my feelings. I didn't know feelings were a gift from God. I didn't know it was okay to feel. Finally, I didn't know I wasn't being honest or real when I pretended to be "fine" to cover my true feelings.

In an effort to help each of us become more honest or real ourselves, we will begin our time together each week by sharing a current feeling with the group. The thought of doing this may bring up some anxiety in you. You may not be used to being so vulnerable. Or, maybe like me, you aren't sure how you feel. My hope is that this group will be a safe place for you to learn what feelings are, how to have them and how to share them.

*How does the thought of sharing your true feelings affect you?*

---

Feelings, what are they? Feelings are our body's response to our belief that our needs are or are not being met. We were created by God, in His image. We were gifted with the capacity to love as well as the ability to feel joy and passion. These positive emotions produce warm, pleasant feelings that cause us to smile, laugh, dance and live life abundantly.

We also have been created with what might be described as "negative emotions". They include anger, pain, fear, shame and guilt. While these emotions can be distressing, they exist to help us know something is wrong, may need our attention, or may need to change. You can consider these to be similar to the warning lights on the dashboard of your car.

God, our Father, has feelings and expresses them throughout scripture.

*What are some of the feelings that God, expresses in the following scriptures?*

    *Genesis 6:6* _____

    *Exodus 34:6* _____

    *Deuteronomy 9:8* _____

    *Deuteronomy 32:21* _____

    *John 3:35* _____

*If you have been created in God's image, can you accept that He gave you feelings?*
_____

Unfortunately, many of us were taught it was not okay to have any emotions or feelings. Often our feelings were met with discipline or rejection. Or we were told that what we felt didn't matter. Many of us learned to survive by denying or stuffing our feelings, limiting our expression of our feelings, or learning to express only positive feelings to stay safe.

Consequently, many of us have no idea how we feel. This is not uncommon. Together we will learn about these parts of ourselves that we have ignored, denied or disowned.

*Do you deny or stuff your feelings or just don't know what you feel?*

_____

## KNOW THE FEELINGS OF YOUR HEART

Knowing the feelings of your heart is important to your understanding of how God has created you, how you function and how to be real. For now we will focus on what feelings are. Later in the study we will talk more about what we are to do with the feelings as we identify them.

*Read and meditate on the definitions of the eight basic feelings on the chart on page 7.*

*What feeling do you least understand?* _____

**Give an example of a time you felt:**

*Anger* _____

*Fear* _____

*Pain* _____

*Shame* _____

*Guilt* _____

*Love* _____

*Joy* _____

*Passion* _____

**What are you currently feeling and why?**

_____
_____

We begin our journey by courageously identifying and honestly sharing our feelings. This is just the first step of becoming the person God created us to be so that we may live authentically with God, ourselves and others.

# FEELINGS

**ANGER:** A strong feeling of **displeasure** caused by an actual or perceived threat to our identity, care, safety or love. Our mental and physical well-being is often directly affected by our resentments/anger. You may be aware of a strong sense of energy or power all over your body if you are angry.

**FEAR:** A strong feeling of **anxiety or apprehension** about a possible or probable event which might cause pain or loss of identity, care, safety, or love. It is often the first thing we feel when we are not in control. You may experience discomfort in your stomach or upper chest if you are afraid.

**PAIN:** An emotional **heartache or suffering** over a perceived or actual loss or harm to our identity, care, safety or love. This can include:

> Sadness - Emotional pain of being unhappy or gloomy due to circumstances.
>
> Self-pity - Emotional suffering because of perception of negative position in life or circumstances. It is often described as feeling sorry for yourself.
>
> Loneliness - Emotional pain due to lack of companionship.
>
> Hurt - Emotional anguish over unmet want or need or loss.

You may sense tightness in your lower chest and heart if you are in emotional pain.

**SHAME:** The pain that results from the perception that **we are fundamentally bad or worthless**. It has to do with perceived identity, not behavior. It often results from some weakness being exposed or as a result of having been abused by another. A synonym for shame is **disgrace**. People who have shame may feel different from others, find it difficult to relax around others, do not want to be the center of attention, need approval of others to validate their value and pretend to be someone other than who they are. Shame can manifest itself in your face, neck or chest as a warm, flushed experience.

**GUILT:** Remorseful, painful feeling which is the result of the belief that one is **responsible for some offensive, wrong behavior or occurrence**. Guilt may be manifested in your gut with a possible gnawing sensation.

**LOVE:** A strong positive emotion of **honor, affection, devotion or worship** toward a person or object. (Strong devotion can also mean idolatry.) Love can often be indicated by a sense of your heart swelling.

**JOY:** A positive sense of well-being, **contentment or blessedness**. It can also mean happy, hopeful or glad. Joy is usually displayed as lightness all over your body.

**PASSION:** A very strong, positive feeling about a person or thing. It can be a strong **motive, enthusiasm or desire** for a belief or action. Passion often manifests itself all over your body as a sense of being energized, excited.

*(Please note: These definitions are paraphrased from several different sources. You may research these more to help your understanding.)*

# STEPS INTO GOD'S GRACE

## LESSON 2: Who Am I?

Are you afraid to make a mistake as a spouse, parent, employee or friend? Are you tired of trying to appear perfect? Are you tired of performing for others' approval? Are you confused about who you are and the true meaning of the life you are living?

For most of my life I wondered how everyone else always seemed to "have it all together" while my life was characterized by failures, broken relationships and unfulfilled dreams. I tried to project an image of perfection and control. I would pretend I was fine and perfect, but inside I was afraid, lonely and hurting. I desperately wanted to be honest, and I often found myself quietly scanning the room for a welcoming face of someone who might desire to be honest too. But all I found were other people pretending to be perfect and expecting the same from me.

Despite my best efforts to keep my mask of perfection in place, sometimes it did slip just a little, and the real, less perfect me was exposed. But I quickly made excuses, denying what had just happened and going on as if everything was once again just "fine". It had become normal to pretend, so normal in fact, that I forgot I was even pretending anymore. Once in a while, however, I still found myself looking for someone who would have the courage to be honest and real.

*Do you ever feel confused about who you are and the meaning of life?*
_____

*Do you pretend your life is "fine" or perfect? Why?*
_____
_____

What if I told you that I have learned that who you are is not about being perfect? It is not about knowing all the right things to do for the right people at the right time. What if I told you that it doesn't matter how well you perform or how good you look or how great your family is? It doesn't matter what other people think of you. What if I told you these things do not define who you are?

*Would you feel disappointed or elated?*
_____

*How would you navigate life differently if you knew for certain that your identity was not determined by your performance, your appearance, your education, or anyone's opinion?*
_____
_____

## IMAGE-BEARER

In my confusion about my identity, I turned to God's Word. As I studied in Genesis, I learned that I was created by God in His image, as are all humans.

We may have forgotten, or maybe we never knew our real identity, but God has never forgotten. Since the time He first created us, His never-ending, never-giving-up, always-pursuing love has been present and active. In His desire to recover those of us who are lost, He pursues us day and night. He calls to us, the broken, blind, weary and lame ones, seeking to draw us into His arms. He knows that if we will rest there and allow Him, He will provide all we need to restore us to our true identity. If we will just ask "who am I?" He will speak the truth to us.

*Read Genesis 1:26-27*

*Who created us?*

_____

*Whose image do we bear?*

_____

*If you could grab hold of the truth of your identity as an image-bearer of God, how would you live each day differently?*

_____
_____

## HUMAN

While we have value and identity as the image-bearers of God, we are not God. God is the one true God who has authority over all things. We have the privilege of being made in His image, but we are not all-powerful, all-knowing, or infinite.

*Read Jeremiah 32:38, Psalm 100:3*

*What is your true identity in these scriptures?*

_____

The definition of "people" is this: human beings, as distinguished from animals. People, humans, are created by God in His likeness, but we are not God.

*How do you feel about being human and not God? Why?*

_____
_____

As soon as God created humans, He gave them directions for living. He blessed them and gave them a purpose. He gave them freedom, but He set boundaries or limits for their authority and actions. He created a garden and placed them there to live. He told them what they could eat and what they could not eat. These boundaries or limits would keep them safe and functioning in the purpose for which they were created.

*Read Genesis 1:28-2:22*

*How did God communicate with the humans He created?*
_____

*What is their purpose?*
_____

*What freedom did God give them, and what are the limits He established for them?*
_____
_____

*How does God's authority differ from that of humans?*
_____

*How did God provide for man?*
_____
_____
_____

God, our creator, established the purpose, limits and freedoms of all humans. Our being real or authentic requires our acceptance of this truth. Our identity, authority and purpose have been established by God alone. We are not God.

*What is your true identity established by God?*
_____
_____

If I allow myself to accept my God-given identity, then I can admit that I do not always know what is best; I cannot do all things; and I do not have authority in my life or the life of others. I am not God. I am a human created by God for a purpose He determined. I am dependent on a power greater than myself (God) for my provision and guidance. **I can stop pretending to be someone I was not created to be.**

*Why might it be difficult for you to accept your God-given identity?*
_____
_____

## MALE/FEMALE

When God created man in his own image, he created them both male and female (Genesis 1:27). Men and women are different in more ways than we can mention here; however, here are some differences you may not know. A woman's metabolism is generally lower than a man's, and a woman has larger kidneys, liver, stomach and appendix but smaller lungs than a man. Men generally have about 40% muscle as compared to 23% for women. Men are more aggressive, combative and territorial than women, who prefer building relationships and helping others. (You probably already knew that!) Women tend to value love, communication and beauty (in addition to relationships), while men value success and respect. The specific variations in gender or its characteristics are not better or worse. They are just different because, while God in His wisdom equipped each of us *differently*, He also equipped us *perfectly* for His intended purposes. (For further reference see www.marriagemissions.com and www.relationship-institute.com.)

*Have you been aware of the extent of the external and internal differences between male/female established by God?*

_____

*How does this affect your judgments and expectations of yourself and those of the opposite sex?*

_____
_____
_____

## LIMITED

Rather than accepting the reality that we are humans created by God, our culture and family of origin have been the strongest influences to determine our identity. Through direct or indirect messages or through words or actions, we have been taught the following:

- We can do anything we want, when we want and how we want.

- We can be all things. We can have all things. We can have a successful career, be a great parent, a giving spouse, loving daughter or brother or friend. We can also serve in the church and community and still have time and energy for "me" and "God".

- We can do all these things if we just try hard enough. We shouldn't need others.

- Love means giving everything away to please others, including our very self, if necessary.

All of these messages convey that we can live without limits for ourselves, other people or things. But most of us can attest that this belief system is not working! We feel overwhelmed, afraid, exhausted; we feel as though we are just not enough. We often fail and disappoint others.

Or others fail or disappoint us. No amount of effort or desire has been able to make up for a lack of time, energy, and ability.

In Romans 1:26 (MSG) Paul says, *"refusing to know God, they did not know how to be human"*. Therefore, in as much as **we have denied the reality that we are not God, we have also denied the truth of our humanity and its limitations.**

Later, in Romans 6:19 (AMP), Paul says, *"I am speaking in familiar human terms because of your natural limitations."* He acknowledges that we are human and limited, even if we do not!

***How have you denied the reality that you are not God and the truth of your humanity and its limitations?***

_____

_____

The human body functions in four basic categories: physical, intellectual, emotional and spiritual. Within these categories, each of us is different, based on how we were created.

**PHYSICAL LIMITS** -- It is important to know needs, strengths and weaknesses of our physical bodies and not ignore or deny this reality.

*Can your body perform without food, water, or sleep?* _____

*Do you have any physical weaknesses?* _____

*What happens if you ignore your weaknesses or over use your strengths?*

_____

**EMOTIONAL LIMITS** – It is important to know how to identify your feelings, needs, desires, values and emotional limits to endure pain, stress, sadness, anger, or joy and passion.

*What do you most desire?* _____

*What motivates you most: love, fear, shame, pain or guilt?* _____

*Give an example of what happened when you exceeded your emotional limits to endure stress.*

_____

**INTELLECTUAL LIMITS** – We do not know all things! Not everyone has the same ability or capacity to process information and retain it. Some people learn by hearing, some by seeing; some people are "big picture thinkers" and some are "concrete, sequential thinkers".

*Do you know all things?* _____

*Do you need to be taught?* _____

*How do you best learn?* _____

*Do you forget?* _____

**SPIRITUAL LIMITS** – In *Surrender to Love,* David Benner writes that to be human is to have been designed for intimate relationship with the Divine. Our spirituality cannot be felt or seen, but it is foundational to our connection to God, ourselves and others. We were created to be in relationship with God and dependent on Him.

*Are you aware of your reality as a spiritual being?* _____

*Do you know all spiritual truth?* _____

*Do you know God or know about God?* _____

*Do you need God? Why?* _____

Hopefully, you are gaining some new understanding about what it means to be human, and that physical, intellectual, emotional and spiritual needs and limitations are inherently part of that identity.

***Given all this new information about your limits, what lies do you believe about your capacity and how do your actions verify these beliefs?***

*Physical*_____

*Emotional*_____

*Intellectual*_____

*Spiritual*_____

*How would your life change if you knew for sure that God created you as a limited being and never intended you to be able to know all, do all and be all--all the time?*

_____
_____

## UNIQUE

We are all children of God, but we are not all the same, no matter how hard we may try to be. In addition to our physical, emotional, intellectual, and spiritual limitations, we have been given unique talents and abilities! *Each of us is an original* (Galatians 5:26 MSG). We have each been created uniquely by God for a specific purpose; therefore, we cannot all do the same things at the same level of competency. *The body isn't just a single part...it's all different but similar parts arranged and functioning together* (1Corinthians 12:14 MSG). We are created differently to function together.

Have you embraced your God-given desires, talents, gifts and abilities, or are you still trying to be who others say you should be…or even who you think you should be?

*What is your passion?* _____

*What are your talents/gifts?* _____

*How do you use them?* _____

*Do you value yours as much as you value those of others?*
_____

## **KNOW THE TRUTH**

We need to get real about the truth of our identity. *We need to recover our identity as image-bearers of God who are unique human beings with physical, emotional, intellectual, and spiritual limits and differences*. We are not infinite. We are not all-knowing or all-powerful beings. We are not God. *We are limited, unique human beings created to live in relationship with an unlimited God.* Our identity is not dependent on *what we do* but rather on *who we are* as humans created by God.

*Do you believe God created you as a human being with unique limitations and giftedness? Explain.*
_____
_____
_____

*Can you accept the reality that you are a limited and unique human? Why or why not?*
_____

*What are the benefits and purpose of:*

   **Being limited?** _____

   **Being unique?** _____

It is our responsibility to know the Truth of who we are. Knowing our true identity we can be better stewards of our bodies as human, male/female, limited, unique and gifted image-bearers.

*Without mentioning what you do, answer the question, "Who am I?"*
_____
_____
_____
_____

# STEPS INTO GOD'S GRACE

## LESSON 3: What is Wrong?

We engage in everyday life as we talk, eat, care for children and work. We look "fine", but unknowingly we are in the grip of a sense of entitlement and an insatiable need for something bigger, better or more than we have. Even worse, we believe we are in control and know what is best. Not surprisingly, we fiercely defend our beliefs and fight against anything or anyone that challenges us or gets in the way of what we want.

What is not visible, but is none the less real, is that we have a deadly disease that is ravaging our bodies, lives, and even our very souls. It is contaminating our thoughts, seeking control of our hearts and actions, all the while leading us on a path of death and destruction.

What is this deadly disease that has been passed down for generations? We will not find the diagnosis in a medical text book. But we will find the Truth by going back to the beginning - the very beginning of mankind.

## IN THE BEGINNING

In Lesson 2, we learned that God created human beings with an identity as His image-bearers with God-given limits, freedoms and purpose. God was the authority and provider. As we continue in Genesis, we observe the condition of the humans when they were created.

*Genesis 2:25:* *"The man and his wife were both naked and felt no shame."*

***What two words in Genesis 2:25 describe the condition of humans when they were created?***

_____

    *Define naked:* _____

    *Define unashamed:* _____

At the time of creation, Adam and Eve were naked and unashamed. However, as we continue our study in Genesis, we will see that Satan's temptation and the actions of Adam and Eve in the garden had tragic consequences on their condition and how these consequences impacted us and all future generations.

## TEMPTATION BY SATAN AND REBELLION OF MAN

*Read Genesis 3:1-10*

*Gen. 3:1 -* *What did Satan's question challenge Eve to consider?*

_____

*Gen. 3:2-3 - How well did Eve remember God's command? What did she add?*

_____

*Gen. 3:5 - What identity did Satan offer to tempt Eve?*

_____

*Gen. 3:5, 6 - Did Eve submit to God's authority and accept her God created identity or take authority to establish her own identity? How?*

_____
_____

Thus in Genesis 3, we see Adam and Eve's rebellion. They wanted to be more than God had created them to be. They wanted to be like God. Adam and Eve chose to exercise their God-given freedom to take authority in their lives and establish their own identity. They doubted God and chose their own way. They ignored God's direction. They depended on what they heard, saw and desired to determine their action. **They had not yet learned to trust God alone.**

*Describe a time you have chosen to exercise your God-given freedom of choice to take authority to establish your own identity.*

_____
_____

*Gen. 3:10 - What did Adam and Eve become aware of after eating the fruit? How did they feel?*

_____
_____

*How did this condition compare with their condition when first created (Genesis 2:25)?*

_____
_____

*Read Romans 1:25*

*What did Adam and Eve exchange, and who did they serve?*

_____

Based on what they *thought* in their minds, *desired* in their hearts and *saw* with their eyes, they *believed* they knew better than God. Adam and Eve traded trust in the true God for trust in Satan and themselves. They disobeyed God, and as a result, sin entered their bodies. They now were aware of their nakedness and were afraid.

*Describe a time when you believed you knew better than God, based on what you saw, felt or thought.* _____
_____
_____

Now aware of their condition, consider what Adam and Eve did to solve their problem, as they perceived it.

*<u>Read Genesis 3:7-13</u>*

*Who <u>**TOOK CONTROL**</u> to fix the problem?* _____

*How did they <u>**COVER THEMSELVES**</u>?* _____

*Who did they <u>**HIDE**</u> from? How?*
_____

*Who did they <u>**BLAME**</u>?* _____

Much like Adam and Eve, we too seek to take authority to establish our own identity and as a result experience shame, guilt and pain. We try to cover ourselves by creating a mask or false image or blame others to hide the reality of our nakedness - our limits, failures and humanity. We are no longer honest or real.

I know I was a master of disguise. For years I attempted to create a false "perfect image" to cover up my limited humanity. I tried to establish my identity in my success at work to cover my insecurity. I hid my emotions to create an image of control, and I said was "fine" to cover my unacceptable emotions of anger or shame. Even if I disagreed strongly, I remained quiet and nodded my head to appear agreeable to cover my fear of rejection. In order to gain others' approval, I said "yes", when I really wanted to say "no". And finally, to protect my perfect image, I blamed others for things that were my responsibility.

***Adam and Eve took control and made fig leaves to cover themselves. We too create a mask to cover our true selves. Describe the mask you have created in an attempt to cover your true human condition.***

_____
_____
_____

*How do you hide from God?*
_____

*Who do you blame for your failures or mistakes or weaknesses?*
_____
_____

Continuing in Genesis, we see God's response to Adam and Eve. *"And terrible pain came into God's heart. His children hadn't just broken the one rule; they had broken God's heart...From now on everything would die...You see sin had come into God's perfect world. And it would never leave. God's children would be always running away from him and hiding in the dark. Their hearts would break now and never work properly again. God couldn't let his children live forever, not in such pain...There was only one way to protect them. 'You will have to leave the garden now,' God told his children, his eyes filling with tears...But before they left the garden, God made clothes for his children, to cover them."* The Jesus Storybook Bible by Sally Lloyd-Jones (pp. 33-35)

*"...the Lord made long coats (tunics) of skins and clothed them. And the Lord God said, Behold the man has become like one of Us (Father, Son and Holy Spirit) to know (how to distinguish between) good and evil and blessing and calamity; and now lest he put forth his hand and take also from the tree of life and eat and live forever--Therefore, the Lord God sent him forth from the Garden of Eden..."* (Genesis 3:21-23 AMP)

**What was God's response to Adam and Eve?**
_____

**Why did God send them from the Garden?**
_____
_____

**How was God's sending them from the Garden an act of love, not punishment?**
_____

Having disobeyed God, Adam and Eve now have the knowledge of good and evil. They know of malice, deceit, slander, jealousy, adultery, coveting and other wickedness. They now have a sin nature. So out of his love for them, God sent them from the garden. Their separation from the garden would protect them from eating of the tree of life and living forever in a sinful, painful condition.

## SIN DISEASE

The question for us is this: What is the effect, if any, of Adam and Eve's sin on the rest of mankind?

**Read Romans 5:12-14 and 7:14**

**Who has sinned?** _____

**What is the penalty for sin?**
_____

**What has every human inherited from Adam and Eve?**
_____

Many of us have been taught through psychology that most, if not all, of our problems, are the result of our family of origin; therefore, we have our parents to blame for our troubles. The truth is, however, that they, like us, also inherited a sin nature. As a result, they may have exhibited many harmful behaviors towards us. But it is not our physical parents' behavior that is the root cause of our most significant problem. **The truth is that Adam and Eve's sin nature has been passed down to <u>all</u> the generations. We inherited it too! Sin contaminates our thoughts, seeks control of our hearts and leads us down a path of pain, destruction and death.**

We, along with everyone else in the world, have inherited a sin nature that makes us a slave to our sinful desires. Keith Miller, in *Hunger for Healing,* calls this a sin disease. This is what is wrong with us. <u>We have a spiritual problem. We have inherited a spiritual disease</u> that is unseen, but whose symptoms are control, selfishness, self-centeredness and fear. It causes us to put ourselves in authority where only God should be and live outside the limits set for us by God. <u>All humans</u> suffer from this deadly spiritual disease!

*What is your spiritual problem?* _____

*Who suffers from this problem besides you?* _____

*What are the symptoms and behaviors of the sin disease or sin nature you inherited from Adam and Eve?*

_____
_____

## I AM A SLAVE

In Romans 7:15 and 7:23 Paul says he discerns how he has been sold into slavery under the control of sin. He is a prisoner or a slave to the sin that dwells in his body. His sin nature makes him do what he does not want to do, and he is powerless to do what he does want to do.

Like Paul, we are a slave to our sin nature that is selfish, self-centered and always striving to put itself in control of our lives and the lives of others. Thinking we know best or believing we have power where we have none, we take actions outside our God-given authority and limits. We are slaves to believing we have responsibility to provide for every need, fix every problem or make others happy or safe. We are slaves to our need to take control, maintain a perfect image or meet others' expectations. We are slaves to our sin nature that propels us to live outside our God-given limits and authority and results in chaos and unmanageability in our lives.

*What do you feel like a slave to, or powerless over? Consider specific people, places, things or situations.*

_____
_____

Up to now, most of us have been unaware or deceived ourselves about the reality of our sin nature and how it functions in our everyday life. We have been unaware of how its keeps our hearts from working properly. We have denied our powerlessness to control it and the unmanageability it causes in our lives and the lives of others. We have denied the truth that we are not in control. We have created masks to hide our imperfections, relied on our performance or things to establish a false, perfect identity, and taken control where we in truth have none. It is time to acknowledge we are powerless to control the sin nature and to admit that our lives are full of frustration, anger, pain, depression and exhaustion.

***How would you describe the unmanageability of your life as the result of the sin nature you inherited from Adam and Eve?***

_____

_____

My life reached its peak of unmanageability after my divorce and during my second marriage. Failing to create a perfect, happy new family from two adults and five children, all with deep hurts and differing needs and expectations, I was exhausted and hopeless. Finally, all of it, combined with the onset of menopause brought me to my knees.

But God heard my cries. He then guided me, through a friend, to an unusual place to find hope and healing: Al-anon meetings. When I first attended the 12 Step recovery program, I read the first step: *We admitted we were powerless over alcohol and our lives were unmanageable.* Though I didn't struggle with alcohol, I knew I was in the right place. I could definitely relate to the idea of powerlessness and the unmanageability of my life, but I felt unsure of how this related to my Christian beliefs. Now having studied Genesis and Romans, I have come to understand that a more biblical statement of this first step is:

**Step One:** *We admitted we were powerless over sin and our lives are unmanageable.*

This first step gave me an understanding of the effects of sin in my life. I lived outside the limits set for me by God; I was controlled by lust, greed, deceit, need for approval, selfishness and fear. My life was unmanageable. It also challenged me to stop pretending, give up the illusion that I was perfect and in control, and I admitted the truth: that I was powerless over sin.

***Are you willing to stop pretending and <u>admit</u> the truth that you are a human being who is powerless over sin (your tendency to live outside the limits set by God) and your life is unmanageable? Why or why not?***

_____

_____

_____

***What new wisdom, guidance or strength have you received as a gift of God's grace toward you as you take this step, admitting you are powerless over sin and your life is unmanageable?***

_____

_____

_____

*Step One Summary to be completed together in small group meeting.*

# STEPS INTO GOD'S GRACE

Step One: *We admitted we were powerless over sin and our lives are unmanageable.*

## 1. The Characteristics of My God-given Identity

Image-bearer _____

Human _____

Male/Female _____

Limited _____

Unique _____

## 2. My Spiritual Problem

I have inherited a _____

I am not free, I am a _____

My future is _____

I live separated from _____

## 3. How My Sin Nature Manifests Itself

I feel _____

I ignore God's authority, take control and trust _____

I cover my limits by creating _____

I hide from God and others by running away to _____

I blame others and things to maintain _____

## 4. How My Life is Unmanageable

When I take control _____

When I try to create a perfect image (mask) _____

When I hide from God or others _____

When I blame others for my limits or mistakes _____

# STEPS INTO GOD'S GRACE

## LESSON 4: Where is Our Hope?

In our previous lessons, we have courageously faced the truth of our identity--not as perfect, all-knowing beings but as created, image-bearers of God with a sin nature, who have rebelled against God. Now knowing the truth of our identity, where do we find hope?

Over the years I used everything at my disposal to try to satisfy my desires and to make my life work. I depended on my thinking, performance, image, other people, money or things for hope. I got temporary fixes from counseling or medication. I tried a new job, new house, and new relationships, even moving to a new city, seeking the help I needed. While some things may have provided temporary comfort, nothing I tried was ever a permanent or life-changing solution.

***What have you looked to in the past for hope or help to make your life work?***

_____
_____

***Have these people, places or things brought the hope you expected?***

_____
_____

My pain and powerlessness created a hunger in me to know God. I was no longer willing to limp along, trying to make life work either on my own, pretending I was God, or depending on the God of my parents or friends. I wanted to put my hope in God, but I needed to know Him better before I could do that. I began asking and seeking. I studied scripture and prayed for insight.

## WHO IS THE GOD OF HOPE?

In Jeremiah 4:22 (MSG) God says, *"What fools my people are! They have no idea who I am!"* The truth is, when we are unable to grasp our identity as humans, we misunderstand God's identity as well. In the opening pages of *Institutes of the Christian Religion*, John Calvin wrote, "There is no deep knowing of God apart from a deep knowing of self and no deep knowing of self apart from a deep knowing of God."

***How has not knowing yourself kept you from knowing the truth of who God is, or how has not knowing God affected your ability to know the truth of who you are?***

_____
_____
_____
_____

*Read Isaiah 44:6 and Deuteronomy 4:39*

*Who is God?*

_____

_____

In the Book of Romans, Paul confesses that while he tried to find hope in his knowledge and self-effort, these were not sufficient to save him from his sin nature. He did not, however, allow his past failures or current experiences to cause him to retreat into self-pity and hopelessness. He immediately rose up and asked, *"Who will deliver me from this body of death?"* (Romans 7:24)

*Read Romans 7:25*

*Where did Paul look for hope?* _____

*Read Psalm 42:5-8 and 43:5*

*Who are we to find hope in?*

_____

*Do you act like God is your only true hope? Why or why not?*

_____

_____

We cannot save ourselves by our own effort to force right thinking, right feelings or right actions. No matter how hard we try, we cannot overcome or fix our spiritual problem. So who will we set our hope on? Who is strong enough, wise enough, powerful enough, and caring enough to save us? Paul says in 1 Timothy 4:10 (AMP), *"We have **fixed our hope on the living God** who is the Savior (preserver, maintainer, deliverer) of all men, especially those who believe, trust and rely on Him."*

We have to give up hoping in our efforts to fix the problems. No amount of striving can fix us or our circumstances. We need to hope in a power greater than ourselves – the living God who is the Savior (preserver, maintainer and deliverer) of all men. The only answer for our spiritual problem is a spiritual solution: God. This is **Step 2:** ***Came to believe that a Power greater than ourselves could restore us to sanity.***

God can be ignored, or He can be known; either way, it does not change the reality of His existence and the fact that our only hope is in Him. God invites us to know Him. He never forces us. God calls us to seek Him. He says we will find Him when we seek Him with all our heart (Jeremiah 29:13). So let us come with open hearts and minds, prayerfully asking, "God, please reveal the truth of who you are to us."

*Write a prayer to God that shares your honest struggles or desires to take Step 2.*

_____
_____
_____

## **WHAT IS THE HEART OF GOD?**

Knowing more information about God was not enough. I wanted to know God's heart. Is He compassionate and loving? Is He good? Does He really care about me and my well-being every day?

These questions took center stage in my mind when I felt deep sadness over the death of someone I loved dearly. He was only 26. He was kind and loving toward all who knew him. Faced with my powerless over death and feeling deep pain and the loss of hopes and dreams, I questioned the character of God. Is God no different than the people who continually disappoint and hurt me? In the midst of my pain, I struggled to know what to believe about God.

***Describe a circumstance that is challenging your beliefs about the character of God.***

_____
_____

The God I knew in my childhood was not enough to sustain me throughout my life. Most times He seemed distant, offering little more than another set of rules for me to follow and imposing unrealistic expectations for my performance. He seemed judgmental and condemning of my failures. I felt alone and abandoned. I viewed Him as a harsh disciplinarian with little or no sympathy for my pain and fear. Yet I tried to force myself to please Him in an attempt to minimize or avoid punishment in this life or eternity. I came to realize that I was relying on my flawed view of God and my limited power to follow a set of religious rules to make my life work. Not surprisingly, neither of them was successful.

***How have your parents, parental figures, spiritual teachers, or experiences influenced what you believe about God's character?***

_____
_____
_____

Instead of relying on what we have been told by others, or maybe what we have made up about who God is, we must go to God himself. God uses all the scriptures to declare who He is, to make himself known to us. He reveals more and more about Himself with each chapter and verse.

In Exodus 33:18-19, Moses asked God to see God. And God said he would make all His goodness pass before him as He proclaimed His name THE LORD.

*Read Exodus 34:6*

*What does God reveal about Himself?*

_____
_____

*Read Psalm 145:7-20 and 146:6-10*

*What does David (a man after God's own heart) declare about God's heart?*

_____
_____
_____

*How might you live differently if you believed this is the heart of God?*

_____
_____

Many of us know or think we know much about God, but not all of it is true. In addition, there is an immense difference between knowing **about** God and **knowing God.** I have learned that my religious knowledge and dependence on rituals and rule-keeping cannot substitute for a relationship with the living God on whom I can depend to do for me what I cannot do for myself.

*Would you say you know <u>about</u> God, or that you <u>know God</u>? Why?*

_____
_____
_____

*Are you hoping that your knowledge and ability to adhere to rituals and rules will make your life work? Or are you hoping in a merciful, loyal, loving God to do for you what you cannot do for yourself?*

_____
_____

We are on this journey together, seeking to know the truth about who God is. By seeking, studying, wrestling and praying over our lifetime, we will come to know the heart of God for ourselves, as David did and expressed so often in the Psalms. As we come to know Him more, we will come to place our hope and trust in Him, for *"Happy is he whose hope is the Lord His God."* (Psalm 146:5)

# **MY HOPE**

When my second marriage was falling apart and my efforts to help my struggling teenagers were failing, I was emotionally exhausted and hopeless. But I felt hopeful as I read Step Two of recovery.

I was able to admit **I was not God.** My life was unmanageable, but my life did not have to be hopeless. When I could finally grasp the reality of my identity and condition as a limited human being suffering with a spiritual disease, I knew my only hope was in the Lord God – a spiritual solution for my spiritual problem!

While in the traditional 12 Steps of recovery we can hope in any god of our choosing, study in God's Word provides the foundation of establishing the only higher power as God the Father, Son and Holy Spirit. He is the One True God. I pray that the Holy Spirit will continue to lead you into an ever deeper understanding of the existence of this power greater than yourself, and that you will *place your hope in His love, grace and mercy toward you.*

***What have you come to know about the character and identity of God, and how has this affected your ability to hope in Him?***

_____
_____
_____
_____

In the next lesson, we will continue our study of Step 2. We will learn about God's plan to rescue each us and why His plan is our only hope for redemption and restoration in this life.

# STEPS INTO GOD'S GRACE

## LESSON 5: God's Rescue Plan

Like most people who are seeking hope and restoration, I turned to religion and its belief system to provide me with some new way of living that would make my life work and free me from my pain and condemnation. I found hope in knowing that God had the power to help me in the midst of my circumstances, but I questioned whether He would, or could, rescue me!

***Do you wonder if God can, or desires to, rescue you from the brokenness and despair in your life? Why?***

_____

_____

## GOD'S RESCUE PLAN

But God had a Rescue Plan for each of us. *"Long before he laid down earth's foundations, he had us in mind, had settled on us as the focus of his love, to be made whole and holy by his love. Long, long ago he decided to adopt us into his family through Jesus Christ. (What pleasure he took in planning this!) Because of the sacrifice of the Messiah, his blood poured out on the altar of the Cross, we are a free people—free of penalties and punishments chalked up by all our misdeeds. And not just barely free, either. Abundantly free! He thought of everything, provided for everything we could possibly need, letting us in on the plans he took such delight in making. He set it all out before us in Christ, a long-range plan in which everything would be brought together and summed up in him, everything in deepest heaven, and everything on planet earth...Long before we first heard of Christ and got our hopes up, he had his eye on us, had designs on us for glorious living, part of the overall purpose he is working out in everything and everyone."* (Ephesians 1:3-12 MSG)

***When did God set His mind on (choose) you and make a plan to rescue you?***

_____

***How would you be adopted into His family?*** _____

***How do you feel knowing God chose you and planned to adopt you?***

_____

As we meditate on these scriptures, we come to know God's heart. He loves us! He never forgot about us! The Truth is He made a plan to provide all that was necessary for the reconciliation of our relationship with Him, redemption of our sin, and freedom from the penalty of death and the slavery to our sin nature. He had a plan to bring us back home to Him, which is the only place we could find happiness and peace!

## NO LONGER SEPARATED, BUT RECONCILED

Because of their sin, Adam and Eve they were sent out of the Garden and away from the presence of God their Father. Because we too have a sin nature, inherited from them, we live separated from God. But God's plan was always to bring us back home to Him. He would do this through His Son Jesus Christ.

*"But God shows and clearly proves His (own) love for us by the fact that while we were still sinners, Christ died for us...we are now justified (acquitted, made righteous, and brought into right relationship with God) by Christ's blood...While we were enemies we were **reconciled to God through the death of His Son.**"* (Romans 5:8-10 AMP)

***How did Christ solve your separation from God?***

_____

_____

## NO LONGER CONDEMNED, BUT REDEEMED

*"All have sinned and are falling short of the honor and glory which God bestows and receives. All are justified and made upright and in right standing with God, freely and gratuitously by His grace (His unmerited favor and mercy), through the **redemption which is (provided) in Christ Jesus**, whom God put forward (before the eyes of all) as a mercy seat and propitiation by His blood (the cleansing and life-giving sacrifice of atonement and reconciliation, to be received) through faith. This was to show God's righteousness, because in His divine forbearance He had passed over and ignored former sins without punishment."* (Romans 3:23-25 AMP)

*"Therefore, there is now no condemnation for those who are in Christ Jesus...God has done what the Law could not do...sending His Son...as an offering for sin."* (Romans 8:1-3 AMP)

This message of redemption through the Savior Jesus Christ was good news for me! This truth brought me hope, for surely I had a past littered with failures and sins that had harmed many. I had learned through many failed attempts that I was incapable of getting myself out of the mess I was in. But Christ's death and resurrection was God's Rescue Plan: a plan to provide a substitute who would pay the penalty for my sins and those of all mankind.

***Define redeem.*** _____

***How did Christ provide a solution for the condemnation for your sin?***

_____

_____

## NO LONGER SLAVES, BUT SONS AND DAUGHTERS

*"But when the proper time had fully come, God sent His Son, born of a woman, born subject to the Law, to purchase the freedom of (to ransom, to redeem, to atone for) those who were subject to the Law, that we might be **adopted and have sonship** conferred upon us (and be recognized as God's sons.)...Therefore, you are no longer a slave but a son..."* (Galatians 4:4, 5, 7 AMP)

*What did Christ come to purchase for us?* _____

*What was our status before Christ ransomed us?* _____

*Once freed, you are adopted as what?* _____

## SONS AND DAUGHTERS STILL HAVE A SIN NATURE

When I understood that through Christ I was redeemed and adopted as God's daughter I was so thankful! But I felt confused: why do I still struggle do the right thing? Why do I still fail and make mistakes? I found my answer as I read about Paul's experience as a believer in Romans 7.

*"I am a creature of the flesh, having been sold into slavery under (the control of sin)...I do the thing I loathe....it is the sin (principle) which is at home in me and has possession of me. For I know nothing good dwells within me, that is, in my flesh. I can will what is right, but I cannot perform it...I endorse and delight in the Law of God in my inmost self (with my new nature) but I discern...a different law (rule of action) at war against the law of my mind and making me a prisoner to the law of sin that dwells in my bodily organs."* (Romans 7:14-23 AMP).

In God's grace, Christ died to be an offering for my sin and to save from me from the penalty of death. His righteousness was credited to me, but **He did not remove the sin nature of my flesh**. I now understand, as Paul did, the spiritual struggle that would continue in me. I could will what was right but I could not carry it out. While, through Christ, I would no longer experience condemnation from God for my wrongs, I would continue to experience a war within me between the sin nature of my flesh and God's truth.

*Did Christ's death and resurrection remove man's sin nature?*
_____

*What conflict would continue to war within all men?* _____

*What does it mean to you to consider that all believers in Christ still struggle with a sin nature?*
_____
_____

# SONS AND DAUGHTERS RECEIVE THE HOLY SPIRIT

God knew that we would still struggle with a sin nature and would need more help. So His Rescue Plan didn't stop at our adoption into His family. He went further. He gave us His Holy Spirit to come live in us!

*"In Him (Christ) we also **were made (God's) heritage** (portion) and **we obtained an inheritance** for we had been foreordained (chosen and appointed beforehand) in accordance with His purpose, Who works out everything in agreement with the counsel and design of His (own) will…In Him you also have heard the Word of Truth…and **were stamped with the seal of the long-promised Holy Spirit.**"* (Ephesians 1:11-13 AMP)

**As part of God's Rescue Plan, what inheritance does God's son or daughter receive?**

_____

God provided an inheritance for His sons and daughters: the long promised Holy Spirit who would empower them to overcome their sin nature!

[God said] *"For here's what I'm going to do…I'll give you a new heart, put a new spirit in you. I'll remove the stone heart from your body and replace it with a heart that's God-willed, not self-willed. I'll put my Spirit in you and **make it possible for you to do what I tell you and live by my commands.**"* (Ezekiel 36:24-28 MSG)

**What would the Holy Spirit make possible for you to do?** _____

*"For it is through Him (Jesus Christ) that we both (whether far off or near) now have an introduction **(access) by one (Holy) Spirit to the Father** (so that we are able to approach Him."* (Ephesians 2:18 AMP)

**What would the Holy Spirit provide?**

_____

*"The Friend, the Holy Spirit whom the Father will send at my request, will make everything plain to you. **He will remind you of all the things I have told you.**"* (John 14:25-26 MSG)

*"When he comes, **he'll expose the error of the godless world's view of sin…he will take you by the hand and guide you into all the truth…he will take from me and deliver it to you**".* (John 16:8-15 MSG)

*"And if the Spirit of Him Who raised up Jesus from the dead dwells in you, (then) He Who raised up Christ Jesus from the dead **will also restore to life your mortal (short-lived, perishable) bodies** through His Spirit Who dwells in you…For if by the power of the (Holy) Spirit you are (habitually) putting to death (making extinct, deadening) the (evil) deeds prompted by the body,*

*you shall (really and genuinely) live forever. For all who are led by the Spirit of God are sons of God."* (Romans 8: 11-14 AMP)

**How else would the Holy Spirit help you?**
_____
_____

The Holy Spirit would teach us how to live. He would guide us and empower us to live rightly as we continued to struggle with a sin nature that wanted to rebel and wander away from God. Only by His power could we win the war between our sin nature (flesh) and God's truth!

## SONS AND DAUGHTERS RECEIVE CITIZENSHIP IN GOD'S KINGDOM

God's sons and daughters, even though they experience all the limitations of sin, inherit citizenship and new life with all its rights and privileges in God's Kingdom today! This Kingdom is a *spiritual* kingdom where Christ reigns as the supreme head of the Church. When Christ returns, He will establish it as a *physical* kingdom. This is all of God's Rescue Plan!

*"But for you who welcome him, in whom he dwells—even though you still experience all the limitations of sin—you yourself experience life on God's terms."* (Romans 8:10 MSG)

*"Therefore you are no longer outsiders (exiles, migrants, and aliens, excluded from the rights of citizens), but you now share **citizenship** with the saints (God's own people, consecrated and set apart for Himself); and you **belong to God's (own) household**."* (Ephesians 2:19 AMP)

**What does the inheritance of sons and daughters also include?**
_____

*"Giving thanks to the Father, Who has qualified and made us fit to share in the portion which is the inheritance of the saints (God's holy people) in the Light. (The Father) has delivered and drawn us to Himself out of the control and dominion of darkness and **transferred us into the kingdom of the Son of His love.**"* (Colossians 1:12-13 AMP)

**God has pursued and delivered His people out of the control of sin and transferred them to whose Kingdom?** _____

*"Here it is in a nutshell: Just as one person did it wrong and got us in all this trouble with sin and death, another person did it right and got us out of it. But more than just getting us out of trouble, **he got us into life**...God is putting everything together again through the Messiah, invites us into life---**a life that goes on and on and on, world without end.**"* (Romans 5:18-21 MSG)

***Besides getting us out of trouble, what did God's Rescue Plan include?***

_____
_____

How amazing is God's love for us that He pursued us and did what we could not do for ourselves. Our Father provided through Christ for forgiveness and healing of our broken hearts and restoration of our relationship with Him! Christ's death redeemed us from condemnation for sin and the penalty of death. Not only are we saved and redeemed, but also we are adopted as God's children. Because of His resurrection, we inherit the Holy Spirit in this life and are given a new, eternal life in the Kingdom of God today.

God had never forgotten about me. His rescue plan would completely solve my spiritual problem. By sending His Son to die for me, He reconciled me to Himself when I placed my faith and trust in Christ. My faith would be credited to me as righteousness. My sins would be forgiven. My relationship with God would be restored! Though I would still have a sin nature, I would no longer be a slave to sin because I would have the Holy Spirit to help me. I would be given a new heart and new life in God's Kingdom today!

***In your own words, write what you understand about <u>all</u> of God's Rescue Plan.***

_____
_____
_____
_____

*"It's news I'm most proud to proclaim, this extraordinary Message of **God's powerful plan to rescue everyone** who trusts him, starting with the Jews and then right on to everyone else."* (Romans 1:16 MSG)

***Describe your feelings as you comprehend the fullness of God's Rescue Plan for you.***

_____
_____
_____
_____

# STEPS INTO GOD'S GRACE

## LESSON 6: Do You Believe?

Knowing of God's love for me and His Rescue Plan for my life gave me reason to hope, but it did not translate into joy in my everyday living. It took time for me to come to confidently believe I was a chosen, redeemed, and beloved daughter of God. It was only by spending time with God on my journey that I was able to grasp the reality of my condition and that He was my only hope in this life!

No wonder Jesus often said *I tell you the truth* before each conversation with His followers. He wanted them to know that they were loved and that God had a rescue plan for them. But they too, much like me, sought answers and listened intently but were confused and found it difficult to believe His words. His ways seemed so different from their ways and His thoughts so different from their thoughts. What He said seemed so impossible to them. Yet, what good was it to them to hear the truth if they didn't understand it and believe it?

## YOU ARE CHOSEN

*"Thus says the Lord, He Who created you...and He Who formed you: fear not for I have redeemed you;* **I have called you by name; you are Mine**. (Isaiah 43:1 AMP) *You are My witnesses, says the Lord, and My servant whom I have* **chosen so that you may know and believe Me and remain steadfast to Me, understand that I am He**. *Before Me no god was formed, neither shall there be after Me."* (Isaiah 43:10, 11 AMP)

As many times as I had heard of God's love, I never embraced the truth that I was intentionally chosen by God to know, believe, and trust Him. I thought I chose Him and that the purpose of that choice was solely for my salvation.

***Do you struggle to believe that God has chosen you? Why?***

_____

_____

## YOU ARE RECONCILED AND RESTORED

God lovingly opened my mind so I could hear and receive the truth of His Rescue Plan. He reminded me that He sent His Son to pay the penalty of death for my sins which would reconcile me with God and restore my relationship with Him. Just by believing this truth I could walk and talk with God once again as Adam and Eve did. I would no longer be alone!

*Read Romans 3:23-25*

***Do you believe the truth that Christ Jesus died to rescue you from sin and death?*** _____

*Read Romans 5:8-10*

*Do you **believe** the truth that your relationship with God has been reconciled and restored? Why?*

_____
_____

*Do you still feel alone? Why?*

_____
_____

Understanding that my relationship with God had been reconciled and restored was an exciting fact, but one I had little real life experience with. People talked about having a personal relationship with Jesus, but I didn't have a clue what that really meant. I knew how to walk and talk with my husband or friends, but I didn't know how to have a personal relationship with an invisible being! As a result, I just continued accumulating information **about** God instead of seeking to **know** God. If I was honest, I didn't really believe that a real day-to-day relationship with Him was available for me.

*Describe your relationship with God.*

_____
_____
_____

## YOU ARE REDEEMED

*"All are justified and made upright and in right standing with God…by the redemption which is (provided) in Christ Jesus…There is now no condemnation for those who are in Christ Jesus."* (Romans 3:24 and 8:1)

Knowing the truth that I was redeemed and no longer condemned did not to sink into my heart. I still struggled with self-hatred for my divorce and my failures in parenting. I still experienced the disapproval or judgment of others for my faults. I still suffered in silence with the weight of my many mistakes.

*Do you believe the truth that you are redeemed?* _____

*What in your life makes you question that you are no longer condemned but redeemed?*

_____
_____

## YOU ARE AN ADOPTED SON OR DAUGHTER

Though I struggled with what redemption and no condemnation really meant for me, I took seriously my new knowledge of forgiveness for my sins and my release of the penalty of death. I diligently applied myself to study my Bible, memorize scripture and attend Sunday school classes. I took to heart the weekly sermons that challenged me to consider what I would do for Christ after everything He had done for me. I served in the nursery, the new member's class, and on the church finance committee. Joining others, I participated in community outreach projects and mission trips. I was determined to exert all my efforts to please God! Wasn't this what God wanted from me? Wasn't I supposed to do something for God after everything He had done for me?

*Read Galatians 4:4, 5, 7*

*Do you **believe** the truth that you are no longer a slave, but an adopted son or daughter of God?* _____

*Does your life reflect more of the characteristics of slave, or of a son or daughter? How?*

_____
_____
_____

I did not apprehend the truth of the whole gospel that through my acceptance of Christ I was adopted into God's family. I failed to grasp that, as a daughter of the King, I did not need to perform for or earn God's love and approval. I was no longer a slave. I was free! I was loved unconditionally. I had never been in a family like that!

*How did the ways of your biological family affect your ability to apprehend the truth of what it means for you to be adopted into God's family?*

_____
_____
_____

## YOU STILL HAVE A SIN NATURE

On the day of my belief in Christ for salvation, I thought I became a new creature who was now perfect and whole. But it seemed to me that no amount of belief in this truth created the life change that I expected. All my performance and service never replaced my unmet longings for significance and love. My wounded heart still ached for peace. I felt guilty and ashamed for my inability to live the Christian life perfectly. What was I missing?

Paul speaks to the Roman believers about his struggle with this same issue. *"What I don't understand about myself is that I decide one way, but then I act another...I need something more! For I know the law but still can't keep it, and if the power of sin within me keeps sabotaging my best intentions, I obviously need help! I don't have what it takes. I can will it, but I can't do it...I've tried everything and nothing helps...I want to serve God with all my heart and mind, but am pulled by the influence of sin to do something totally different."* (Romans 7:15-25 MSG)

While I had embraced God's Rescue Plan, I could see that my sin nature was still very present and active. It continually sought to control my mind, heart and actions. No matter how hard I tried to make the right choices and make myself into a good Christian, I still struggled with anger, failure and fear. I still yelled at my children. I often failed to meet the expectations of my parents or spouse.

***Do you <u>believe</u> that even as a Christian you still have a sin nature?*** _____

***What in your experience validates this belief?***
_____
_____

***Do you feel you need more help?*** _____

## **YOU HAVE RECEIVED THE HOLY SPIRIT**

God knew we needed more help too. Even though Christ would die, He said He would not leave us alone. He would send us the Holy Spirit to provide the help we needed for everyday life.

<u>*Read Ephesians 1:11-13*</u>

***Do you <u>believe</u> the truth that, as a son or daughter, you receive the invisible presence of God Himself, the Holy Spirit, to live in you? Why?***
_____
_____

*"But if **God himself has taken up residence in your life**, you can hardly be thinking more of yourself than of him. Anyone, of course, who has not welcomed this invisible but clearly present God, the Spirit of Christ, won't know what we're talking about. **But for you who welcome him, in whom he dwells – even though you still experience all the limitations of sin – you yourself experience life on God's terms.** It stands to reason, doesn't it that if the alive-and-present God who raised Jesus from the dead moves into your life, he'll do the same thing in you that he did in Jesus, bringing you alive to himself? When God lives and breathes in you (and he does, as surely as he did in Jesus), you are delivered from that dead life."* (Romans 8:9-11 MSG)

God's Word said that even though I would experience all the limitations of sin, the helper would transform me from the inside and strengthen me to live in God's ways. Sadly, because I did not comprehend the immense power and presence of the Holy Spirit, I had little or no experience with God's supernatural gift or its power and strength for me.

*Describe your experience with the Holy Spirit in your life.*

_____

_____

## **YOU HAVE NEW LIFE IN GOD'S KINGDOM TODAY**

*"Jesus went all over Galilee... teaching people the truth of God. God's Kingdom was his theme- that **beginning right now they were under God's government**, a good government! He also healed the people of their diseases and of the bad effects of their bad lives."* (Matt 4: 23-25 MSG)

*"God's Kingdom is wherever God is King...wherever God is in charge...where He fills your heart up with His Forever Happiness....Coming home to God is as wonderful as finding a treasure ...being where God is – being in His Kingdom – that's more important than anything else in all the world. God is real treasure." The Jesus Storybook Bible* by Sally Lloyd-Jones (pp. 250, 255)

Jesus proclaimed, "God's Kingdom is here!" Beginning right now new power and new ways are in operation. God did what the Law and the people were not able do! God would be our strength, power, and provider. He would chase away our enemies and heal our broken hearts. This was all part of our inheritance in God's Rescue Plan!

***Do you believe that right now God's Kingdom is here?*** _____

***Do you believe you have new life in God's Kingdom today as part of God's Rescue Plan? Why?***

_____

_____

*"Can you imagine the breathtaking recovery life makes, sovereign life, in those who **grasp with both hands this wildly extravagant, life-gift**, this grand setting-everything right, that the one man Jesus Christ provides? Here it is in a nutshell: Just as one person did it wrong and got us in all this trouble with sin and death, another person did it right and got us out of it. But **more than just getting us out of trouble, he got us into life!**"* (Romans 5:17-18 MSG)

***Do you believe that Jesus came to give you real life and abundant life today?*** _____

I believed God's message that salvation and redemption through Christ was God's way to get me out of trouble for my sins, but I didn't have a clue about the new, wildly extravagant life. What was Paul talking about? I couldn't imagine a different kind of life was available in the here and now. Because I had retained a life of self-dependence, in bondage to self-effort, I didn't have any experience with the Holy Spirit and a free life or a better life. I was a Christian, but the reality of my life was far from "abundant", and I felt very little freedom or joy. Not understanding the fullness of God's Rescue Plan through Christ, I was still watching and waiting.

*Do you consider your life to be one of freedom and joy, better than you could have ever imagined? Why?*

_____
_____

*When you consider God's Rescue Plan for you, what struggles do you have in hearing, understanding and believing in it fully?*

_____
_____
_____

## STEP TWO: CAME TO BELIEVE GOD CAN RESTORE ME

I was not aware of the existence of the spiritual Kingdom of God where Christ is reigning as King. Failing to understand my inheritance as God's Child, I was ignorant of the presence, purpose and workings of the Holy Spirit to guide me and form Christ in me. I did not know or believe the fullness of God's Rescue Plan and, clinging to my beliefs that I could through my own efforts I could know all, do all and be all, I did not look for or perceive a need for God. I chose to retain my illusion of control; I deceived myself into thinking I was more than I was, and I rebelled against God. But I came to believe the truth: *I can't; but God can.*

*Are you coming to believe that only The Lord God, His Son Jesus Christ and the Holy Spirit can rescue you and restore you to sanity? Why or why not?*

_____
_____
_____
_____

This is **Step Two:** *Came to believe that a power greater than ourselves can restore us to sanity.* In taking this step I had to admit that knowing about God's Rescue Plan was not the same as believing it. God's Rescue Plan would not do me any good if it was not mixed with my belief. Finally, the truth of this Step, my life and God's Word came together.

  1) My true identity is a limited, human being. I am created by God and struggle with a sin nature.
  2) Christ is the true King of God's Kingdom; His is the only true power.
  3) I need God to rescue me from the insanity of my life.

*Have you taken Step 2 and come to believe that God can restore you? Why?*

_____
_____
_____

# STEPS INTO GOD'S GRACE

## LESSON 7: King of My Kingdom

As I came to know more of the truth of who I am, who God is and His Rescue Plan for me, I began to see that these truths were disconnected from my everyday life. While I had professed belief in Christ for forgiveness of my sins, I still suffered from despair and discouragement. My life was characterized by pain, anxiety, guilt and shame. Where were the abundant life and rest that Jesus promised me?

I boldly brought my complaint before God. In His gentle but honest response, He spoke into my heart: "Maybe it's time to look at the truth about your life from My perspective. Your resistance to authority began to show itself during your childhood. When you became an adult, you decided you would no longer be told what to do and when to do it. From then on, you made up your mind that you would decide what was best, and you would be in charge. You declared yourself king in the kingdom of your heart. Later, even though you accepted My free gift of Christ for salvation and eternal life, you ignored My Holy Spirit, and you chose to continue to live in rebellion to my authority. You believe Christ is your Savior, but you do not believe He is your King. You have not turned your life over to Him."

***How have you continued to live in rebellion while saying you believe?***

_____

_____

_____

## MY REBELLION

I was humbled by God's words to me. They were difficult to hear, but I knew in my heart they were true. I believed that I could establish my own authority and create and maintain my own identity and image, as well as the image I expected of others!

God then led me through a process of looking at how things worked in my life in "My Kingdom," where I was the self-appointed king. This included naming some of the beliefs/rules in "My Kingdom" that I thought everyone should live by. After I honestly acknowledged these beliefs/rules, I listed the feelings I had as a result. Then, as best I could, I listed the actions I took in response to my feelings to maintain control and enforce the rules in "My Kingdom." God helped me see the results.

***Review the following page which represents much of the truth about life in "My Kingdom". Ask God and your sponsor to show you how things work in Your Kingdom. Then complete the worksheet provided.***

# MY KINGDOM

### MY BELIEFS/RULES

1) I am king and I have authority over my life and the lives of others who live in my kingdom.
2) My wisdom is sufficient to plan my way and the way of others.
3) Happiness is my right.
4) I depend on myself to make life work.
5) God's job is to give me what I want to make me happy.
6) Freedom comes from doing what I want, when I want, and how I want.

### MY FEELINGS

1) I live in fear of not getting the things I want.
2) I live in fear that I will lose what I have.
3) I am angry at myself and others who do not give me what I want.
4) I am angry at God because He is not giving me what I want.
5) I am angry at others because they expect me to give them what they want.
6) I feel shame for not being enough.

### MY ACTIONS

1) I ignore God's authority and take control to try to get what I want or to protect what I have.
2) I cover my limits and imperfection by creating a mask or false identity.
3) I hide by running away to shop or work and defend my kingdom at all cost.
4) I blame and criticize others for not meeting my expectations and needs.

### MY RESULTS

1) I fail to meet my expectations for my life.
2) I am condemned by others for my failures.
3) I am exhausted from trying to increase my levels of performance to reach a place of acceptance, significance and success.
4) I am frustrated by a life that is not meeting my needs for happiness, love, and significance.
5) I question God's love for me.

## _____(Your Name)_____'s KINGDOM

**MY BELIEFS/RULES** (that everyone in my kingdom should live by)

1)

2)

3)

4)

5)

6)

**MY FEELINGS** (that result from my beliefs/rules)

1)

2)

3)

4)

5)

6)

**MY ACTIONS** (taken to enforce my rules or in reaction to my feelings)

1)

2)

3)

4)

5)

**MY RESULTS** (success, failure, outcome)

1)

2)

3)

4)

5)

Once I placed myself on the throne, the selfish, controlling behaviors of my sin nature caused failure and chaos! As king, I relied solely on my limited thinking and abilities to provide for myself and others living in My Kingdom. It was a kingdom based on of self-determination, self-reliance, self-improvement, self-preservation, and self-effort. I worked very hard to create the perfect life for myself and my subjects. I exerted all my efforts to make them into who I thought they should be, which included control of what they ate, how they dressed, what they did for a living, so they would have a good life. I was often angry or resentful because they didn't seem to appreciate my efforts. I responded by blaming them because I believed I was just trying to help and, in fact, I knew what was best! Even if confronted about the error of my ways, I was powerless to stop telling others what to do. I continued to control and manipulate at every turn. If I failed, I just tried harder to do the same things and blamed God for not helping me!

As you reflect on "Your Kingdom", consider these questions.

***As a limited king, how do you try to maintain an illusion of control in your kingdom?***

_____

_____

_____

***How do you feel as king of your kingdom?***

_____

***How do think others in your kingdom feel?***

_____

***How successful are you as a king?***

_____

***Has rebelling and placing yourself as king in your kingdom been effective to produce your desired results? Why?***

_____

_____

_____

I now see how I rebelled against God and challenged His authority. I appointed myself as king and reigned in My Kingdom. I rejected Christ's authority as the true king and ignored the power and presence of the Holy Spirit. These were the greatest obstacles to my ability to experience the abundant life of rest and peace that Christ promised. I was exhausted from taking authority to put myself in control over people, places and things that God never intended me to control. I could relate to what Keith Miller said in *Hunger for Healing*: "I finally saw that to replace an all-loving, powerful, affirming and wise God with my own self-centered and self-destructing will can certainly qualify in itself as an act of insanity."(p. 40)

*"People knew God perfectly well, but when they didn't treat Him like God, refusing to worship him, they trivialized themselves into silliness and confusion so that there was neither sense nor direction left in their lives. They pretended to know it all, but were illiterate regarding life."*
(Romans 1:21-22 MSG)

**How have you known about God but not treated Him like God?**

_____

_____

We did not treat God like God. We placed ourselves in authority in our kingdoms, lived by our will and experienced lives that were unmanageable. It is only with an understanding of this truth that we are ready to humbly consider **Step 3: *Made a decision to turn our will and our lives over to the care of God as we understood Him.*** In the next two lessons, we will consider God's invitation to surrender as kings in our kingdoms, and make a decision to assume our rightful position as God's son or daughter in His Kingdom.

**How do you feel as you consider surrendering control of your kingdom in Step 3?**

_____

_____

_____

# STEPS INTO GOD'S GRACE

## LESSON 8: Will You Rebel or Surrender?

God revealed that my greatest act of rebellion was establishing myself as king in my kingdom. I said I believed Christ died for my sins and trusted Him for my salvation and eternal life, but I followed the ways of the world more than God's truth. I ignored God's presence and challenged His authority. Believing I knew best, I took for myself the authority that belonged only to Him. Taking control of my life and the lives of others, I depended on money, my thinking, or my ability to make life work and get what I wanted.

I was one of the *"people (who) draw near to Me (God) with their mouth and honor Me with their lips but remove their hearts and minds far from Me, and their fear and reverence for Me."* (Isaiah 29:13 AMP).

I was one of the rebel children who *"make plans, but not mine (God's)"* (Isaiah 30:1 MSG).

I was one who *"claimed to know God, but by their actions they deny him"* (Titus 1:16).

I was a rebel, and my rebellion was worse than I could have imagined!

*Are you a rebel against God? How?*

_____
_____
_____

I spoke about God. But I did not believe His words nor revere or respect His authority in my life or in the lives of others. My heart was more connected to my children, husband and my work than to God's heart. I was unwilling to accept my limited humanity. I was stubborn and unyielding in my desire to control. **I was more comfortable seeking God in a book than surrendering in complete dependence on Him in real life!**

*How do you feel about your rebellion against God?*

_____
_____

At first it was hard to acknowledge the reality of my resistance and defiance. But as this truth worked its way into my heart, I wept for my arrogance and my rebellion against God. I realized that as a rebel and king of my kingdom, I carried the responsibility to fight many battles to defend my kingdom. My weapons were often ineffective and my skills limited. I lost more battles than I won, but I never gave up. Every day brought a new battle, and every day I fought harder to defend and provide for myself and my subjects. But one day, when my arms and legs were weary, my wounds seemed life-threatening, and my skills could not save me or those I loved, I was willing to raise the white flag of surrender. I was tired of feeling lost and alone. I was tired of trying to win against insurmountable odds. I was at the end of my rope. I couldn't fight the battles any longer.

*Are you tired of being king? Are you at the end of your rope? Why?*
_____
_____
_____

## GOD'S INVITATION: WILL YOU SURRENDER?

Often at the end of a battle, a more powerful force demands the surrender of the other who has less power. **But God invites; He never forces us.** He graciously reminds us of His sovereignty. *"Yours, O Lord, is the greatness and the power and the glory and the majesty and the splendor, for everything in heaven and earth is yours. Yours is the kingdom, you are exalted as head over all."* (1 Chronicles 29:11 NIV)

*Who is the rightful king?* _____

Then, out of His mercy and love, He offers an invitation to His rebel children who have been unwilling to listen. *"Your salvation requires you to turn back to me and stop your silly efforts to save yourselves. Your strength will come from settling down in complete dependence on me – the very thing you've been unwilling to do."* (Isaiah 30:15 MSG)

*What is God's invitation to His rebel children?*
_____
_____

*How do you feel about this invitation?*
_____
_____

*Do you believe your strength will come from complete dependence on God or yourself? Why?*
_____
_____

*Have you settled down in complete dependence on God? Why?*
_____
_____

The concept of complete dependence became clearer as I read Paul's instruction to the believers in Rome: *"So here's what I want to do, **God helping you**; Take your everyday, ordinary life--your sleeping, eating, going to work and walking around life--and place it before God as an offering. Embracing what God does for you is the best thing you can do for him. Don't become* *so well-adjusted to your culture that you fit into it without even thinking. Instead, fix your attention on God. You'll be changed from the inside out."* (Romans 12:1-2 MSG)

***Can you surrender on your own?*** _____

***Who helps you surrender?*** _____

***How does fitting into the culture make it difficult to believe and surrender control to God?***
_____
_____

***What parts of your sleeping, eating, going to work life and walking around life do you most want to surrender control of to God? Why?***
_____
_____

***What parts of your sleeping, eating, going to work life and walking around life do you not want to surrender control of to God? Why?***
_____
_____

***Are you willing to ask God to help you surrender? Why?***
_____
_____

## ACCEPT THE SOVEREIGNTY OF GOD

I struggled with the concept of surrender and trusting God. I live in a country that exalts democracy – government by the people, for the people to have freedom and liberty! From childhood my culture encouraged me to be self-reliant and live by self-effort. I had little experience with someone ruling over me.

Moreover, I was afraid of what surrender would mean for my future. I wanted assurances from God. "Can't you prove to me that you are trustworthy before I surrender," I asked. He responded, "Surrender, then you will know that I am trustworthy."

***What assurances would you like from God before you surrender?***
_____
_____

Truthfully, I wanted more than just assurances from God. I wanted a conditional surrender; one where I still had some control over what I believed was important or my responsibility. But God had a different kind of surrender in mind for me. It was the same unconditional surrender that preceded God's blessing of Abraham as the father of many nations; a surrender that resulted in travels to unknown lands and sacrificial offering of his son Isaac.

*"Abraham entered into what God was doing for him, and that was the turning point. He trusted God to set him right instead of trying to be right on his own....But if you see that the job is too big for you, that it's something only God can do, and you trust him to do it--you could never do it for yourself no matter how hard and long you worked--well, that trusting-him-to-do-it is what gets you set right with God, by God. Sheer gift...**The one who trusts God to do the putting-everything-right without insisting on having a say in it is one fortunate man.**"* (Romans 4:3-9 MSG)

*Those who are **people of faith are blessed** and made happy and favored by God (as partners in fellowship) with the believing Abraham.* (Galatians 3:9 AMP)

**What is God's promise for people of faith (those who believe)?**
_____

**Do you see the job is too big for you?** _____

**How do you feel about surrendering and trusting God to put everything in your life right, without having a say in the outcome? Why?**
_____
_____

## YOU ARE BLESSED WHEN YOU SURRENDER

*(Jesus) sat down and taught his climbing companions. This is what he said: "You're blessed when you are at the end of your rope. With less of you there is more of God and his rule. You're blessed when you feel you've lost what is most dear to you. **Only then can you be embraced by the One most dear to you.** You're blessed when you're content with just who you are – no more, no less. That's the moment you find yourselves proud owners of everything that can't be bought.* (Matthew 5:1-5 MSG)

**Are you at the end of your rope? Why?**
_____
_____
_____

**Do you feel blessed when at the end of your rope (poor in spirit) or when you have lost all that is dear? Why?**
_____
_____

*What does Jesus say happens when*

    *There is less of you?* _____

    *You feel you've lost what is most dear?* _____

    *You are content with just who you are?* _____

Jesus said we are blessed to be at the end of our rope and feel like we have lost all that is dear, because this drives us to God's Kingdom. If we will believe Him, surrender and stop trying to get and do, we will experience God's giving. Then we will know God's reality and God's provision. We will find all our needs would be met.

***Do you believe Jesus? Why? Why not?***

_____

_____

## STEP 3: WILL YOU SURRENDER YOUR KINGDOM?

I said I believed in Christ for salvation, but I did not trust Him and give Him complete authority in my everyday living. My surrender had conditions. I was still busy building my own kingdom and justifying its existence, believing I was building it for God on God's truth. But God was asking me to stop building my kingdom and offer Him my complete surrender. He was asking me to turn over all my sleeping, eating, everyday life to Him.

It was then I came face to face with **Step Three:** *Made a decision to turn my life and my will over to the care of God.* One again God was inviting me to make a decision to recognize His sovereignty and turn over my life and will to Him.

In A Hunger for Healing (p. 51), Keith Miller says *"When I came to this step* (Step 3) *I thought I had already surrendered because I'd verbally given God control of my life; I was confused. I said, "There's something wrong here, because I've done this "turning my life and my will over to God" in church, in evangelical meetings and now I'm supposed to do this again in a Twelve-Step program?" Yet somewhere inside I knew my faith was not working. I could not seem to stop overcommitting and working all the time, and I was compulsive in many areas of my life. And yet I prayed every day for relief and change. I could not understand why my prayers were not being answered, because I knew I'd be able to serve God better if my compulsive and addictive behavior were stopped."*

In Homesick for Eden, Gary Moon wrote, *"I had been born again so many times my soul had stretch marks! But I had no personal experiential knowledge; no personal experience with the kingdom…The concept of abundant life was nothing more to me than words on the page…."*

***How often have you said the words "I surrender"?*** _____

*Do you have any experience with the abundant life?* _____

Turning my will and my life over to the care of God was more than giving God some of my time by going to church and bible studies. It was more than prayer or service in the nursery. It was surrendering as king in my kingdom, to give God authority <u>all</u> areas of my life. It was giving Him my hopes, my dreams, my plans for myself and my plans for others. It was trusting Him for direction in my life and waiting for His provision. This unconditional surrender was the only way for me to move from a life of chaos as king of my kingdom to a life of peace. To gain my life I had to lose it! (Mark 8:35)

***What is the only way for you to move from a life of chaos to a life of peace?***
_____

***How is <u>this</u> surrender different from other times you may have surrendered to God?***
_____
_____

***What hopes, dreams, and plans are you afraid to surrender to God?***
_____
_____
_____

Jesus said, *"You have your heads in your Bibles constantly because you think you'll find eternal life there. But you miss the forest for the trees. These Scriptures are all about me! And here I am, standing right before you, and you aren't willing to receive from me the life you say you want."* (John 5:39-40 MSG)

*"For I know the thoughts and plans I have for you, says the Lord, thoughts and plans for welfare and peace and not for evil, to give you hope in your final outcome."* (Jeremiah 29:11 AMP)

*"Do not be like the horse or the mule, which lack understanding, which must have their mouths held firm with bit and bridle, or else they will not come with you. Many are the sorrows of the wicked, but he who trust in, relies on, and confidently leans on the Lord shall be compassed about with mercy and with loving-kindness."* (Psalm 32:9-10 AMP)

***As you consider your rebellion and God's invitation to surrender, how do these words of scripture impact you?***
_____
_____
_____

# STEPS INTO GOD'S GRACE

## LESSON 9: Receive New Life in God's Kingdom

God provided all that was necessary for my recovery and restoration through Jesus and the Holy Spirit. If it seemed that my spiritual problem was not being resolved or I was not experiencing a more abundant life, it was not because God has not done enough. It was because I had not understood and surrendered to all that Christ accomplished. In My Kingdom, I felt more comfortable living by sight and in rebellion, so I had not surrendered and embraced the reality of His spiritual kingdom and power for me today.

But when I said, "I believe, I want to surrender and turn over my life to you Lord," God led me to read John 10: 9-10 (AMP). Jesus says, *"I am the Door; anyone who enters through Me will be saved (will live). He will come in and he will go out freely and will find pasture....I came that they may have and enjoy life and have it in abundance (to the full)."*

**What does Jesus say we will find when we enter through the door He opened?**
_____

*"Strive to enter by the narrow door, for many, I tell you, will try to enter and will not be able."* (Luke 13:24)

As I read these words, God revealed that the door was narrow. When I was puffed up with pride and arrogance, living in rebellion, I could not enter. Only when I made the decision to surrender I was able to go through the narrow door Jesus had opened into a new life in God's Kingdom! Surrender was the only way for me to enter.

**Do you believe Jesus has opened the door <u>for you</u> to new life?**
_____

**How do you enter the door to new life?** _____

## EMBRACE THE MYSTERY OF LIFE IN A SPIRITUAL KINGDOM

Studying and seeking to know more of this new life in God's Kingdom, I read *"To you it has been given to (to come progressively to) know (to recognize and understand more strongly and clearly) the mysteries and secrets of the kingdom of God..."* (Luke 8:10 AMP)

Reading this scripture, I realized that God chooses those to whom He intends to reveal the mysteries of His Kingdom. These mysteries and secrets are only known by divine revelation, often cannot be fully understood and must be accepted by faith. That is why they are mysteries and secrets! Because I had a tendency to reject anything I could not understand, I ignored or rejected the mysteries and secrets God wanted to reveal to me as His child.

*Do you find it difficult to embrace mystery and secrets of a spiritual kingdom? Why?*

_____

_____

*"We have not ceased to pray and make (special) request for you, (asking)* **that you may be filled with the full (deep and clear) knowledge of His will** *in all* **spiritual wisdom** *... and the understanding and* **discernment of spiritual things**...*and that you may be invigorated and* **strengthened with all power** *according to the might of His glory."* Colossians 1:9-11 (AMP)

*"I pray to God...that He may grant you a* **spirit of wisdom and revelation (of insight into mysteries and secrets) in the (deep and intimate) knowledge of Him***, by having the eyes of your heart flooded with light, so that you can know and* **understand the hope to which He has called you***, and* **how rich is His glorious inheritance in the saints***. And (so that you can know and understand) what is the immeasurable and unlimited and surpassing greatness of His* **power for those who believe***, as demonstrated in the work of His mighty strength."* (Ephesians 1:17-19 AMP)

Finally, in Colossians 1:26-27, Paul says his purpose is *"to make the word of God fully known...the* **mystery of the saints which is: Christ in us***!"*

**What are some of the mysteries and secrets of God's Kingdom?**

_____

_____

_____

_____

*How many of these mysteries have you believed or experienced?*

_____

_____

_____

As a "beginner" in the life of faith, I lived in ignorance of the mysteries and secrets of new life in the Kingdom and the fullness of the presence of Christ in me. As a result, I had no experience with an intimate relationship with God. I had no wisdom or discernment of spiritual things and no experience with God's power for me.

I am thankful that Christianity is unlike other religions which require their disciples to know and keep the rules imposed on them by others. No! God's Rescue Plan provided all the help I needed to understand His truths and live by them. The One I sought to worship and follow came to live inside me to help me! The Holy Spirit (Christ in me) would reveal the mysteries of God's Kingdom to me <u>and</u> empower me to live by them!

I was not left alone by God to live life as best I could until I die and go to heaven. Jesus made the way for me to be adopted into God's own household and, as His child, to receive my inheritance in my present life and for eternity. I just needed to surrender, embrace the reality of "Christ in me" and receive the mysteries of His Kingdom by faith.

*Are you willing to surrender and embrace the mystery of the saints? Why? Why not?*

_____

_____

Humbly, I realized that just as the Jews had failed to recognize the living physical presence of Jesus with them, I had failed to recognize the spiritual presence of Christ in me (the Holy Spirit) and my "sonship" in His spiritual Kingdom today.

*How might you live differently if you apprehended the full mystery of "Christ in you"?*

_____

_____

## **ASSUME SONSHIP**

By surrendering my kingdom and apprehending this truth of "Christ in me", I assumed my position as God's daughter living in His Kingdom. Then I began to experience the Holy Spirit teaching me, guiding me and empowering me to live there!

*"And if the Spirit of Him Who raised up Jesus from the dead dwells in you, (then) He Who raised up Christ Jesus from the dead will also **restore to life your mortal bodies through His Spirit Who dwells in you**...But if through the power of the (Holy) Spirit you are (habitually) putting to death the (evil) deeds prompted by the body, you shall (really and genuinely) live forever. For **all who are led by the Spirit of God are sons of God**."* (Romans 8:11-14 AMP)

*Who are led by the Spirit?* _____

*What will the Spirit do?* _____

Over time, **little by little**, with the Holy Spirit's help, the mysteries and secrets of God's Kingdom became less mysterious. I began to know God's voice, know God's will and walk in His ways. As I listened and followed, the Holy Spirit was transforming me on the inside. With only my willingness and without my effort or His force, I found myself becoming more loving, patient, kind, compassionate and able to endure suffering. The fruits of the Spirit were the outflowing of my renewed mind and new heart restored by God alone. All I did was surrender and trust Him to do it. This trusting allowed the mystery of "Christ in me" to work.

*What mystery of God's Kingdom is becoming less mysterious to you? Why?*

_____

_____

# RECEIVE NEW LIFE IN GOD'S KINGDOM

*"This resurrection life you received from God is not a timid, grave-tending life. It's adventurously expectant, greeting God with a childlike 'What's next, Papa?' God's Spirit touches our spirits and confirms who we really are. We know who he is, and we know who we are: Father and children. And we know we are going to get what's coming to us—an unbelievable inheritance!"* (Romans 8:15-17 MSG)

God wanted to give me my inheritance in His kingdom. But I couldn't receive all of my inheritance until I surrendered and gave up living as a rebel king in my kingdom. My surrender allowed me to walk through the door that Christ opened and into new life in God's Kingdom where my heavenly Father welcomed me home into His loving arms and protective embrace. **Then I realized my salvation wasn't only for the purpose of giving me eternal life in the hereafter; it was the beginning of a whole new life, here and now, living as a daughter in God's Kingdom!**

***Do you believe the Father wants to give you the kingdom?*** _____

***Are you willing to receive it? Why?***

_____

_____

I began to seek a better understanding of what God's Kingdom was like. Based on the truths of God's Word and the revelation of the Holy Spirit, I gained spiritual knowledge and wisdom regarding the **whereabouts of this Kingdom, who is really king, and the ways of living the King has set for us to live as His children.**

***Read through the next page entitled "God's Kingdom." Meditate on the mysteries and secrets of God's Kingdom and pray for God's Holy Spirit to give you insight, wisdom and willingness to live in the truth of His Kingdom.***

# GOD'S KINGDOM

*Now is come the salvation and the power and the Kingdom of God and the authority of Christ.* (Rev. 12:10)

## GOD'S TRUTH

1) The Kingdom of God does not come by visible display; it is within you (in your hearts). (Luke 17:20-21)

2) God is the First and the Last. There is no other God. He is good to all and has all power, authority and control. (1 Chronicles 29:11; Isaiah 44:6; Psalm 145:9)

3) Jesus is God's Son who died for man's sins, to redeem them from the penalty of death and reconcile them to God. (Mark 14:61-62; Romans 5:8-10)

4) I am a limited, unique human, created by God. I have a sin nature. Through faith in Christ I am forgiven and adopted as God's son and heir. The Holy Spirit lives in me. (Genesis 1:26-27; Romans 5:8-14; Galatians 4:4-7; Ephesians 2:19; Colossians 1:27)

5) The Holy Spirit is the Spirit of Truth sent by the Father. (John 14:16-17)

6) The most important law is to love the Lord your God with all your heart, all your soul, and all your mind; and love your neighbor as yourself. (Matthew 22:36-40)

## MY ACTIONS (if I believe these truths)

1) I live by faith. (Galatians 2:20)

2) I seek God's Kingdom, trust in His Word, and hope in His ways. (Matthew 6:33; Psalm 119:42-43)

3) I am led by the Holy Spirit (Christ in me). (Romans 8:14)

## ACTIONS GOD TAKES

1) God keeps truth and is faithful. He executes justice and lifts up, protects, preserves and defends us. (Psalm 146:6-9)

2) God restores life to us through the Spirit. (Romans 8:11)

3) God works all things together for our good and molds us into the image of Christ. (Romans 8:28-29)

4) God imprints His laws on our minds and engraves them on our hearts. He acts with mercy and grace toward us. (Hebrews 8:10-12)

## GOD'S RESULTS (PROMISES)

You shall be comforted, satisfied, receive mercy, see God, be called sons (and daughters), inherit the kingdom, and be the light of the world. (Matthew 5:1-14)

*All scripture references are from the Amplified Translation.*

*What new information have you learned about God's Kingdom?*
_____
_____
_____

*How do you feel about what you now know about God's Kingdom?*
_____
_____

*Compare life in your kingdom from Lesson 7 to life in God's Kingdom to answer the following questions:*

1) *Who has authority in your kingdom? In God's Kingdom?*
_____
_____

2) *What do you depend on to guide you in your kingdom? In God's Kingdom?*
_____
_____

3) *What does it mean to live by self-effort in your kingdom versus by faith in God's Kingdom?*
_____
_____

4) *How do your actions in your kingdom compare to God's actions in His Kingdom?*
_____
_____
_____

## **LIVE WHAT YOU SAY YOU BELIEVE**

When I compared the insanity of my kingdom with the promises of God's Kingdom, my fears around the mystery of surrendering to an invisible God with an invisible Kingdom lessened. I now saw that the familiar way, living as king in my kingdom where I walked alone in rebellion and self-effort, only led to exhaustion, condemnation, failure and frustration. But there was another path, one that could only be entered by my surrender. It was an unknown path, but it promised an inheritance of new life in God's Kingdom.

*What are the two paths that are presented before you?*
_____
_____

Consider these mysteries and secrets:

1) You have "Christ in you!"
2) You are citizens and sons/daughters in God's Kingdom.
3) Your home is in God's Kingdom, which is presently an invisible, spiritual kingdom that is not of this world. You are in the world, but not of the world.
4) God alone has all authority and power. Christ is your king.
5) God's children accept the sovereignty of God in all areas of life, know God's truth, follow the Holy Spirit and live by faith.

***Which is most difficult for you to trust and rely on? Why?***

_____
_____
_____

When I chose to surrender and go through the door that Christ opened, I found the new life I had been missing. I began to know God's voice, to receive wisdom beyond my understanding, to experience healing of my wounded heart and to know peace and joy in the midst of trials. My faith grew from a faith in the death of Christ for my sins to include faith in the risen Christ to give me a new life of wisdom, restoration, healing, and provision for today and every day! I was ready to take **Step 3:** ***Made a decision to turn my life and my will over to the care of God.***

***Do you believe Jesus died for your sins?*** _____

***Are you willing to take Step 3 and make a decision to surrender your life and will into the care of God? Why?***

_____
_____
_____
_____

Congratulations! You have received the Truth that God wants you to know! Now prepare to begin your new life in God's Kingdom. It will be a life full of mysteries, healing and restoration as the Holy Spirit leads you in the Way God wants to transform you.

# STEPS INTO GOD'S GRACE

## PART TWO: THE WAY GOD WANTS TO TRANSFORM ME

> *But religion—the well-intentioned efforts we make to get it all together for God—can very well get in the way of what God is doing for us. The main and central action is everywhere and always, what God has done, is doing and will do for us....Our part in the action is the act of faith...we don't get in the way but on the Way.* (*The Message* by Eugene Peterson, Introduction to the Book of Hebrews)

# STEPS INTO GOD'S GRACE

## LESSON 10: Led into the Way

Our journey, so far, has been filled with God's grace and favor. He has opened our minds to know the Truth of our identity as limited humans with a sin nature and the magnitude of our rebellion--pretending to be God and living as kings of our kingdoms. He revealed the fullness of His Rescue Plan and invited us to unconditionally surrender our kingdoms, receive our inheritance and live in His Kingdom. It is not enough for us to know this Truth. We must learn to live according to the Ways of His Kingdom where God is our authority, His Word is the Truth and His Holy Spirit is our guide.

As kings of our kingdoms, we depended on our sight, hearing and mimicking skills to learn how to live. We figured life out on our own, mostly learning by trial and error. We watched what others said or did, and then we tried to copy their behavior. We often were punished when we acted wrongly and ignored or rewarded when we acted rightly. This is how we learned how to live and how I taught others to live.

***What specific skills did you depend on as king in your kingdom to make life work?***

_____

_____

But now, we live in God's Kingdom, and God has entirely new ways of living and different kind of training in mind for us. In His Kingdom, we do not have to depend on our thinking to figure out how to live in our new home. We will each be personally taught by God! He will teach us the Way and empower us to walk in it!

*Jesus said, "You're not in charge here. The Father who sent me is in charge...**I do my work, putting people together, setting them on their feet**, ready for the End. This is what the prophets meant when they wrote, 'And then **they will all be personally taught by God**.' Anyone who has spent any time at all listening to the Father, really listening and therefore learning, comes to me to be taught personally – to see it with his own eyes, hear it with his own ears, from me, since I have it first from the Father."* (John 6:43-46 MSG)

*"I still have many things to tell you, but you can't handle them now. But when the Friend comes, the **Spirit of the Truth, he will take you by the hand and guide you into all the truth** there is."* (John 16:12, 13 MSG)

***Describe your experience of being personally taught by God or guided into all truth by the Holy Spirit.***

_____

_____

# INTO THE WILDERNESS

You are about to embark on the adventure of your life! The Holy Spirit who led the Israelites and Jesus Christ into the wilderness will now take you, another of God's chosen ones, into a spiritual wilderness, where you will cultivate a new life with God. God will personally teach you more of the Truth of who you are, who He is and the Way to live in His Kingdom.

*"Blind eyes will be opened; deaf ears unstopped, lame men and women will leap like deer…springs of water will burst out in the wilderness, streams flow in the desert. …There will be a highway called the Holy Road. No one rude or rebellious is permitted on this road. It's for God's people exclusively –impossible to get lost on it…Only the redeemed will walk on it. The people God has ransomed will come back on this road. They'll sing as they make their way home…"* (Isaiah 35:4-8 MSG)

On the Holy Road in the wilderness, you will visit the Oasis of Examination, the Mountain of Confession, the Valley of Repentance, the River of Forgiveness, and the Pathway of Peace. At each of these places you will stop and personally experience God's divine provision and blessing for you, which will help transform you into the image of Christ.

***Where are you going and why are you going there?***

_____
_____
_____

***How do you feel about the journey that lies ahead?***

_____
_____
_____

There are five important principles to practice while on your journey in the wilderness:

1. ## FOLLOW THE HOLY SPIRIT WITH AN OPEN MIND AND WILLING HEART

    Let the Holy Spirit decide where you will go. Instead of claiming to know what to do, ask, *"How do we understand God in this?"* (Jeremiah 23:35 MSG) Offer an open mind and willing heart to allow Him to guide you to places where your deepest beliefs and values will be examined. Your capacity to endure difficulty will be stretched. Your ways of manipulating and controlling, which may have served you well as king in your kingdom, will not be profitable for you here. You must learn to be led, guided and counseled by the Holy Spirit.

    *Thus says the Lord, "**I'll take the hand of those who don't know <u>the way</u>**, who can't see where they're going. I'll be a **personal guide to them, directing them through unknown country**. I'll be right there to show them what roads to take, make sure they don't fall into the*

*ditch. These are the things I'll be doing for them...not leaving them for a minute."* (Isaiah 42:14-16 MSG)

***Who leads you on the journey into the wilderness, and what do you offer?***

_____

_____

2. **HAVE COURAGE IN THE FACE OF FEAR**

The Holy Spirit has led me to unusual places in my wilderness journey, many of which I would not have chosen for myself. A recovery 12 Step group was one of those places. Often I found myself wondering what I was doing there in a room filled with hurting people who spoke a language I did not understand. I often wanted to run away. It seemed too frightening to be around people I didn't know, talking about things I didn't want to hear, feeling things I didn't want to feel. I wanted to retreat back into the safety of my known, well-worn path of life, even if it was chaotic. Willingness and resistance battled within me much of the time. I thought I was too weak and wounded to make such a journey. But the way to healing and restoration is through fear, not around it!

***What are your thoughts or feelings as you consider the journey ahead?***

_____

_____

The Holy Spirit kept confirming, "This is the Way, walk in it." As I followed, God provided all I needed through His Word, the Holy Spirit, my sponsor who had been on the journey before me, and my fellow strugglers. I was strengthened, encouraged and even excited about what lay ahead.

*"Fear not, for I am with you; do not look around you in terror and be dismayed, for I am your God. I will strengthen and harden you to difficulties, yes, I will help you; yes, I will hold you up and retain you with My right hand of rightness and justice."* (Isaiah 41:10 AMP)

***Who or what has God provided to help give you courage to take the journey?***

_____

_____

3. **ALLOW THE HOLY SPIRIT TO TEST, SEARCH AND EXAMINE YOU**

In the wilderness, we welcome the light of God's truth and His Holy Spirit into our minds and hearts. It is not is not a harsh process, but a loving one. Because God cares deeply for us, He slowly and gently reveals the lies that we believe. He shows us our unhealed wounds and the idols we worship. His purpose is to help us see the truth of our condition and then free us and heal us of anything that keeps us in bondage and fear, living as a child of man.

*"The heart is hopelessly dark and deceitful, a puzzle that no one can figure out. But **I, GOD, search the heart and examine the mind**. I get to the heart of the human. I get to the root of things. I treat them as they really are, not as they pretend to be."* (Jeremiah 17:9, 10 MSG)

**Can anyone figure out our heart and mind?** _____

**Have you tried to figure them out?** _____

**Who alone can search the heart and mind of the human?** _____

**What is God's purpose for the examination?**
_____
_____

4. **HAVE AN ATTITUDE OF MERCY AND GRACE**

   When we recognize the truth of our sin nature and the failures or brokenness that result, we no longer seek to hold ourselves or others to an unattainable standard of perfection. We have a new attitude. We rely on God to help us respond with mercy and grace, not condemnation and punishment. *"For there is now no condemnation for those who belong to Christ Jesus."* (Romans 8:1)

   **How does your attitude in the wilderness differ from how you have previously responded to failures and harms?**
   _____
   _____

5. **ALLOW THE HOLY SPIRIT TO IGNITE THE KINGDOM LIFE IN YOU**

   *"The main character in this drama will **ignite the kingdom life within you**, a fire within you, the Holy Spirit within you, changing you from the inside out. He's going to clean house– make a clean sweep of your lives. He'll place **everything true in its proper place** before God; **everything false he'll put out** with the trash to be burned."* (Matthew 3:11-12 MSG)

   **What does the Holy Spirit do to change you?**
   _____
   _____

   Once we know the extent of the contamination of our minds and hearts by our sinful nature and the ways of man, we allow the Holy Spirit to change us from the inside, to ignite His Kingdom life within us! We will not choose our way, but we will allow the Holy Spirit to show us the Way. Out of this life will flow grace, mercy and love toward ourselves and others.

*For here's what I'm going to do: I'm going to take you out of these countries, gather you from all over...pour pure water on you and scrub you clean.* **I'll give you a new heart; put a new spirit in you. I'll remove the stone heart...replace it with a heart that's God-willed,** *not self-willed.* **I'll put my Spirit in you** *and* **make it possible for you to do what I tell you and live***...You'll be my people and I'll be your God.* (Ezekiel 36: 22-36 MSG)

***What does God promise to do to solve the problem of our hopelessly dark, deceitful heart and mind?***

_____

***Do you trust God to fulfill these promises?*** _____

God's plan includes making everything in us new. He doesn't just patch us up. He gives us a new heart and a new spirit that will make it possible for us to mature and grow as His child. Our new heart will be more yielded to God and will allow Him to put everything in its proper order for His children. A renewed mind and new heart will make it possible for us to follow God's Ways.

## 6. <u>LEARN THE WAYS OF LIVING IN GOD'S KINGDOM</u>

In the wilderness, the Holy Spirit will work to teach us God's ways and transform each of us from a child of man into a child of God. We will learn the practice of examination to help us know our minds and hearts and the power of confession to break the bonds of deception and shame. Then, with the help of the Holy Spirit, we will repent of our old ways of thinking and living and ask God to remove the idols we worship more than Him. We will learn how to put on the Armor of God every day to protect and defend us as we go forward to love. When we have completed our journey, our minds will be full of God's thoughts, our hearts motived by God's love. We will know God's ways and how to live by them, on earth and in heaven.

*For My thoughts are not your thoughts, neither are your ways My ways, says the Lord...* (Isaiah 55:8 AMP)

***What will you learn in the wilderness? Why do you need to learn this?***

_____

_____

_____

_____

## <u>EXPECT A MIRACLE</u>

God longs to have His children walking in intimate relationship with Him. He longs to give us His Kingdom. But when we lived as kings in our kingdoms, relying only on our abilities to control and fix outcomes, we were not receiving from God all He desired to give us.

*But whoever did want him, who believed he was who he claimed and would do what he said,* **He made to be their true selves, their child-of-God selves**. (John 1:12-13 MSG)

As I embraced my identity as God's Child living in a strange new kingdom, I found it easier to trust God and accept my need to be taught God's mysterious ways of living. I learned to know the Holy Spirit's voice and accept Him as my personal tutor and friend. I learned He was always with me, and His job was to point out, with mercy and grace, where I thought wrongly or acted with malice. I learned He would reveal the meaning of God's Word to me and convey God's love for me.

As I came to believe God would do what He said He would do, and trusted Him to do it, I experienced acts of His divine power doing for me what I could not do for myself. God delivered me from the darkness of shame and guilt from past sexual sins. He freed me from the debilitating fear of rejection and need of others' approval. He healed much of the pain in my heart from harms and losses in my past. He gave me a new life that was better than any I could have imagined. I am so thankful that the Holy Spirit, my sponsor, and my companions on the journey firmly held my hand. They helped me go through my fears so that I could begin to receive the healing and restoration of my true self, my child-of-God self!

**What miracle or act of divine power do you hope will come from God on this journey?**

_____

_____

**List the names of all those whose hands you will hold tightly as you take this journey.**

_____

If you are willing, you can join me and other children of God who are walking on the Holy Way– the Way of following the Holy Spirit and trusting God. The Holy Way is through the wilderness. It is there you will learn the spiritual practices of examination, confession, repentance and forgiveness. The Way will help restore you as a Child of God and help you cultivate an intimate relationship with your heavenly Father.

Fortunately, you are not alone. Hold tightly to your companions' hands. Listen as Holy Spirit reminds you of the Truth of who you are and who God is. Listen as He teaches you the mysterious ways of living in God's Kingdom, and trust that He cares for you and will never leave you or forsake you. Welcome to the wilderness, where you will begin experiencing the supernatural power of God in your life!

# STEPS INTO GOD'S GRACE

# LESSON 11: The Oasis of Examination

Welcome to the wilderness where we will begin our radical new life with God! Our first stop is the Oasis of Examination. Plan to stay here awhile, settle in and unpack your belongings. Lay down your agendas and plans. Rest and discuss your journey so far with your companions. Share more of your questions and struggles. Then as you come to know each other more deeply, strengthen and encourage each other. Separated from the busyness and noise of the rest of the world, give your undivided time and attention to God.

## THE BLESSING

God has taught you the truth of your identity. You are a human, created in the image of God. Now, as you take the fourth step of your journey, you will come to know the truth of how God created you to function, the limitations of your humanity, and the effects of sin and separation from God on your life. You may not be aware of why this is important for you now, but as the Holy Spirit opens your eyes and you come to understand this truth, you will see that it impacts everything you do, and every relationship in your life!

*"I am not conscious of anything against myself, and I feel blameless; but ...it is the Lord (Himself) who examines and judges me...for He will both bring to light the secret things that are (now hidden) in the darkness and disclose and expose the (secret) aims (motives and purposes) of hearts."* (1 Corinthians 4:4-5 AMP)

So settle in at the Oasis of Examination. You have divine appointments with the Holy Spirit, and it is critically important to learn to discern His voice over your own as He teaches you what it means to be human. Allow Him to give you a clearer picture of the reality of your limits, the effects of sin on your mind, heart and actions. TRUTH is His blessing for you here. *You will know the truth, and the truth will set you free.* (John 8:32)

***How can the practice of self-examination give you a clearer picture of your limits and the effects of sin?***

_____

_____

_____

## YOUR FIRST DIVINE APPOINTMENT

In your study of Genesis, you came to know the truth of who you are and who God is. You learned that you are created by God, as a limited human, to live in relationship with Him. Now, in your first appointment at the Oasis of Examination, open your eyes, ears and mind as the Holy Spirit reveals the Truth of how God created you to function.

# THE HUMAN MIND

Humans were created with a mind that is the control center of the body. The thoughts and beliefs in the mind affect the heart and cause our actions! There are, however, limitations to the functions of the human mind. Instead of striving against these limitations in our own strength, God intended to teach and guide us into truth.

1. ## THE MIND GATHERS INFORMATION

    From the time we were born, we seek to understand our surroundings, other people, and how life works. We survey our environment and take in information through our God-given physical senses of smell, touch, sight, taste and sound. We incline our minds to gather information from many sources, including school, media, parents, and other people. Knowing that our mind gathers data is helpful, but what is most important for us to know are the limits of the mind to gather data!

    a. What we can know is limited by the human body's intellectual and physical capacity to take in and retain information. We were not created with ability to know all things.
    b. Information in our mind is limited to the data we are exposed to through our senses.
    c. The mind often cannot discern between real or imagined data. For example, often the body responds with feelings of fear to a violent event in a movie as if it were happening to you directly.

    ***In what ways have you experienced your minds limited ability to gather information?***
    _____
    _____

    ***How might these limitations affect the reliability of the information in your mind?***
    _____
    _____

2. ## THE MIND ASSIGNS MEANING, CREATES BELIEFS AND IMAGINES OUTCOMES

    God created the human mind with a capacity to reason (understand) or assign meaning to the information it gathers. Based upon our assigned meaning or assumptions, the mind creates a thought and belief system. This system becomes our limited perception of reality. *Incline your mind to understanding.* (Prov. 2:3 AMP)

    But it is essential for us to note that these thoughts and beliefs we perceive to be true are based on:

    a. The quality and quantity of limited data our mind is capable of gathering;
    b. Our limited reasoning capacity;
    c. Any faulty assumptions, others' opinions, and past experiences;
    d. Our inability to know the future.

*When have you trusted the meaning you assigned or a belief you created, and it turned out to be false?*

_____

_____

*How might these limitations affect your ability to trust the meaning you assign or the outcomes you imagine?*

_____

_____

3. **THE MIND DECIDES AND DIRECTS ACTION**

Once our mind assigns meaning or imagines an outcome, it decides on a course of action and then directs what we will say or do. *"The mind of a man plans his way ...."* (Prov. 16:9) But these decisions and directions are limited by:

a. The accuracy of our perception of reality;
b. The actions our mind and body have already learned.

*Give an example of a time you took action based upon your assigned meaning and imagined outcome, only to discover you were wrong.*

_____

_____

4. **THE MIND LEARNS**

Thoughts, beliefs, and actions are created, recreated or modified by the mind to allow the human body to learn and adapt to its environment as necessary to insure survival and improve our lives. *"Learn to do right!"* (Isaiah 1:17) Over time, thought patterns are strengthened by repetition and become part of our subconscious. As the mind learns and thought patterns are strengthened, "automatic" decisions and actions result. What we learn, however, has limitations.

a. What is learned is limited by our intellectual capacity.
b. Once we have learned something, it is often difficult to change our minds, even in spite of contradictory information.
c. Much of our learning occurs when we were children with limited reasoning ability.
d. Learning is limited by quality and quantity of information gathered, meanings assigned, and results of previous actions taken.

*Give an example of when the limitations of what your mind had learned negatively affected your life.*

_____

_____

## 5. THE MIND REMEMBERS AND FORGETS

The mind remembers or stores the details of past situations in the form of memories, which can be recalled for future reference. What the mind remembers determines whether we will choose to duplicate or avoid similar situations in the future. What and how much we remember are limited:

a. Memories are only formed from limited information gathered, limited meaning assigned, actions taken and consequences experienced. *I remember the days of old...*(Psalm 143:5)
b. Many painful or traumatic memories are stored so deeply we cannot access them without help from the Holy Spirit.
c. The mind does not remember every detail, nor does it remember every circumstance. It often forgets information as we age or as new information is added.

***When have you experienced the limitation of your human memory?***

_____
_____

It's hard to believe how long I blindly went through life, gathering information, assigning meanings that were false and imagining outcomes that never happened. Unfortunately, these misperceptions or falsehoods were the foundation for decisions I made and actions I took. Neither questioning the process nor the reliability of the data produced in my mind, I always trusted my thinking. With the help of God's Word and the Holy Spirit, I was shocked to learn the truth of how my mind functions and how limited it really is.

***What truth have you discovered about how your human mind functions, its power and its limitations?***

_____
_____
_____

***What is the most surprising characteristic of your human mind? Why?***

_____
_____

## THE HUMAN HEART

The heart was created to work in concert with our mind and God's will. It represents the center of our desire, or will, which gives us the ability to trust and motivates us into action. It also has a God-given ability to feel a range of emotions, including fear, pain, joy, sadness, guilt and love. The heart is directly impacted by what the mind <u>believes</u> to be true.

1. **DESIRES OF THE HUMAN HEART**

   Our desires are the internal power, or "want to," that motivates us to make a decision and then take action. When coupled with the perception of reality in our mind, our desires affect how we feel and cause how we behave.

   God fashioned the heart of man with desires that would motivate him to seek God and follow His will. *Delight yourself also in the Lord and He will give you the desires and secret petitions of your heart.* (Psalm 37:4 AMP)

   After study of scripture, discussions with many people and my own experiences, I have learned much about the desires in our hearts. In an attempt to keep things simple, I have condensed our God-given desires into the following categories:

   a. **Identity** - Identity encompasses the characteristics and values that describe us as an individual. Our identity consists of knowing who we are, including an awareness of our uniqueness, strengths and weaknesses. Our original God-given identity was human; a child of God created in His image.
   b. **Provision** - Provision is a supply for the needs of our mind, heart, body and spirit. A desire for provision encompasses needs for food, sleep, water, clothing, housing, exercise, and rest. It may also include a desire for knowledge, physical comfort, emotional well-being, spiritual help and a need for significance. God intended to be our provider.
   c. **Protection** - Because we are vulnerable and frail, we need protection from harm. We need emotional, financial, physical or spiritual security. God intended to be our protector.
   d. **Love** - God is love. Therefore, He created us with a desire to love and be loved. Love includes acceptance, intimacy, or close personal attachment. God intended to be our primary source of love.
   e. **Purpose** - We each have a God-given, unique purpose for our life, intended to work in conjunction with His other Children, to bring His will and kingdom to earth.

   *Which of the God-given desires of your human heart is the most powerful motivator in your life? Least powerful?*

   _____
   _____

   *Has a lack of awareness of these God-given desires affected your life? How?*

   _____
   _____
   _____

2. **FEELINGS OF THE HUMAN HEART**

   God gave us hearts that have the ability to feel as God feels. Feelings indicate the state of our emotional, spiritual or physical condition and motivate us to take action. Without feelings we would live as robots, mechanically going through the motions of life, disconnected from God, ourselves and others:

a. **Love** allows us to grow in an intimate relationship with God, self and others.
b. **Passion** energizes us to fulfill God's plan and purpose for our life.
c. **Joy** emerges from a sense of inner peace, not outward circumstances.
d. **Anger** warns us that our needs, or God's desires, are not being met. It can motivate us to fight against injustice.
e. **Fear** warns us of our need for God's protection or provision, or to turn in another direction.
f. **Guilt** convicts us of actions that lie outside God's limits and motivates us to repentance.
g. **Pain** provides opportunities for God to comfort, teach and train us. It motivates us to move in another direction or depend on God.
f. **Shame** warns us that we have forgotten our identity as a beloved, limited Child of God. It motivates us to turn to God and forgive ourselves.

*What have you misunderstood about the function of the feelings of your heart?*
_____
_____

*When have you acted out of your feelings and caused harm?*
_____
_____

## HUMAN ACTIONS

We were created with a physical body that has the ability to take actions which flow from responses to our needs and desires. Lovingly, God molded our minds, hearts, hands, feet, mouths, and eyes to express His compassion and mercy and carry out His will. We were intended to be vessels of His love and entrusted to care for His creation. Our unique gifts and abilities would help us work together to fulfill God's purpose and plan. God intended to direct and fulfill **our desires, create or maintain our identity and purpose, provide for our protection and provision, and give us love.** God's plan for the actions to be taken by humans is as follows:

1. We are to have dominion: to establish His kingdom. *"Be fruitful, multiply and fill the earth and subdue it; and have dominion over the fish of the sea, the birds of the air, and over every living creature that moves upon the earth."* (Genesis 1:28-29 AMP)
2. We are to work under God's direction and keep the garden. *"The Lord God took the man and put him in the Garden of Eden to tend and guard and keep it. And the Lord God commanded the man..."* (Genesis 2:15-16 AMP)
3. We are to help one another. Man and woman were fully exposed to each other, naked and without shame. *"And the rib the Lord God had taken from the man He built up and made*

*into a woman, and brought her to the man....and the man and his wife were both naked and were not embarrassed or ashamed in each other's presence."* (Genesis 2:22-25 AMP)

4. We are to work together in harmony to fulfill His purpose and plan. *"The body isn't just a single part...it's all different but similar parts arranged and functioning together."* (1 Corinthians 12:14 MSG)

***Who has authority over your actions, and what actions did God direct you to take as a human?***

_____
_____
_____

Before I understood my mind's function and its powerful effects on everything I felt or did, I wrongly assumed I had the ability to know all things. I believed my feelings were based on fact. Unaware of the connection between my mind and heart and my need for God, I trusted what I believed and failed to balance reason with feelings. Too often, I let my feelings control my actions instead of letting God control them. I followed my feelings more than God, which caused me to struggle in life and relationships. As I have gained more understanding of my limited humanity and the way I was created to function, I am more aware of my need for God in my life!

***Take some time to consider what you have learned about the limits and functions of your mind, heart and body. What blessings of Truth have you received? How might this truth affect your life?***

_____
_____
_____
_____

***What has this shown you about your need for God?***

_____
_____

(Please note: Next week you will begin the examination process. Please give yourselves significantly more time each week to read and complete the assignments in Lessons 12, 13 and 14.)

# STEPS INTO GOD'S GRACE

## LESSON 12: At the Oasis: Inventory-Part One

At the Oasis, we have an opportunity to take the next step of our journey. We hear the Holy Spirit's invitation, "Come, *let us examine and test our ways and let us return to the Lord."* (Lamentations 3:40) Here He will help us test our minds and hearts to reveal the reasons why we struggle.

The first time I was invited to examine and test my ways, I was afraid of what it might reveal. I now know that examination is not to be feared, but welcomed! It fact, it was one of the most life-changing experiences of my life! *The Lord helps them and delivers them; He delivers them…because they trust and take refuge in Him.* (Psalm 37:40 AMP)

**How do you feel about the Holy Spirit's invitation to examine and test your ways? Why?**

_____
_____

## STEP FOUR—INVENTORY

The way of examining ourselves begins **with a searching and fearless moral inventory. This is Step 4.** The word 'inventory' means to record the facts which describe someone or something. Many of us have taken an inventory of what is in the pantry or the garage. In this case, with the help of the Holy Spirit, we will take an inventory of ourselves.

The Holy Spirit, who knows how God made us, will help us look at our mind, heart and actions to reveal if we are functioning as God intended. He will help us consider our relationships to identify our beliefs and desires. He will help us carefully examine our scars and wounds. The goal of the examination is not to cause us additional shame or pain, but only to identify what needs to be restored or redeemed for God's glory and our joy!

**What will be revealed at the Oasis and why?**

_____
_____

## SPONSOR AND COMMITMENT

The process of examining yourself is unfamiliar and may at times be difficult. Since you cannot see yourself by yourself, this series of lessons on Step 4 is best if entered into with the help of a sponsor! A sponsor is someone you trust who has previously completed a 12 Step Study. A Sponsor can provide additional strength and wisdom to help you to see yourself honestly. Please take time to identify and ask someone to be your sponsor at this time, if you have not already done so.

*Who is your current sponsor, or who have you asked to sponsor you?*

_____
_____

While you have the help and support of the Holy Spirit, your personal understanding of this Step will only come as you make a commitment to the time and effort necessary to complete the inventory over the next few weeks.

*What changes are you willing to make in your life right now to help provide the additional time and effort necessary to take this step?*

_____
_____

## YOUR SECOND DIVINE APPOINTMENT

During your second divine appointment, you will begin your inventory by considering your relationships. It is through the examination of relationships that patterns of thinking, feeling and acting will be revealed. By first identifying the people with whom you struggle (WHO), you can then articulate the circumstances of these struggles (WHAT). Once these struggles are identified, you will inventory the beliefs in your mind (WHY). In the next Lesson, you will examine the other reasons why you struggle: the desires and feelings of your heart and the actions you have taken (WHY). (Refer to MY INVENTORY form at end of lesson)

*How is <u>this process</u> of self-examination different from self-examination you may have done in the past?*

_____
_____

*What questions or concerns do you have about this process?*

_____
_____

The process of examination will help you know truth about yourself that may have been unknown by you. I suggest you begin by praying *"that God would grant us a spirit of wisdom and revelation (insight into the mysteries and secrets) in the (deep and intimate) knowledge of Him, by having the eyes of my heart flooded with light, so that you can know and understand the hope to which He has called you, and how rich is His glorious inheritance in the saints. And (so you can know and understand) what is the immeasurable and unlimited and surpassing greatness of His power in and for us to believe, as demonstrated in the working of His mighty strength."* (Ephesians 1: 17-19 AMP)

# INVENTORY: PART ONE

The primary purpose of this lesson is to help you understand the inventory process and begin your inventory. Please work with your sponsor to complete a comprehensive inventory.

*Before you continue with the Lesson, stop here and make a copy of the MY INVENTORY form and EVE'S INVENTORY form at the end of this lesson and place them before you. Now you are ready to continue.*

# WHO

In the WHO column of MY INVENTORY, you will record the people in your life with whom you struggle. Generally, this is someone who, when they come to mind, causes some discomfort, possibly feelings of anxiety, anger, guilt or shame. These are people who may have harmed you, or whom you harmed. Write down their names. Harms can be physical, emotional, financial or social. If you struggle with yourself because of some of your choices in life or blame yourself for harms to others, write down your name. If you struggle with God for any reason, including not giving you the life you expected, write down His name.

To help identify people with whom you might struggle, ask yourself the following questions:

a) Who made an unwanted change in my life or harmed me?
b) Who confused me or betrayed me?
c) Who forced me to do something I didn't want to do?
d) With whom did I feel unsafe or unloved?
e) Who told me "no"?
f) Who was I unable to say "no" to?
g) With whom did I have interactions that cause me to feel shame or guilt?
h) Who do I think about, or talk about, in a negative way?
i) Who failed to meet my expectations or disappointed me?
j) Who do I not want to see or go with to dinner?

To help with your understanding of this process, read in Genesis 3 Eve's encounter in the Garden of Eden, and consider WHO she struggled with. Did someone tell Eve "no"? The answer is **God**. Did someone confuse Eve? Yes, the **Serpent and herself**! These are the names listed under WHO on EVE'S INVENTORY.

*Now begin your inventory. Make several copies of the MY INVENTORY form. Find a quiet place. Pray. Then, ask yourself the questions indicated above to help you identify a person or persons with whom you struggle. Write down names of persons that come to mind under WHO.* It may help to consider your life in segments: childhood, adolescence, early adult, adult, marriage, career or parenthood, etc. At a minimum, list one person from your childhood, one as an early adult and one from your current life to help you see the patterns of thinking, feeling and acting that have developed over your lifetime. If you have done a complete inventory of your life previously, you may consider doing an inventory on a specific person or event which still troubles you today.

## WHAT

After listing the names of people with whom you struggle under WHO, move across to WHAT. In this column, describe the facts of the struggle. This is what you saw, heard, or experienced. At this time, do not write about any thoughts or feelings. List as many specific incidents that come to mind that relate to each WHO on your inventory worksheet. If you were hurt, describe the situation or the nature of each loss. The following are examples to help you know what to write under WHAT to describe your struggle with another person:

a) Spoke manipulative, harsh or critical words to me when_____
b) Took harmful actions towards me when _____
c) Did not support, help, appreciate or agree with me when _____
d) Left me alone when_____
e) Told me "no", punished me, or forced me when _____
f) Didn't listen to me or follow my direction when_____

If you listed your name under WHO, describe the nature of your inadequacy, failure or loss under WHAT.

Now go back and look at Eve's Inventory. Notice the facts of her circumstances under WHAT. She struggled with God because He set a limit for her. He told her she could not eat from one of the trees. She struggled with the Serpent because he enticed her with the possibility of being like God if she ate the one fruit God had told her not to eat. Finally, she struggled with herself because she was confused about what to do. The fruit appeared good in her eyes, but God said not to eat it and the Serpent said she could eat it.

*Returning to your inventory, use the suggested statements above to help you describe the circumstance related to the person you listed under WHO. Write the facts of the circumstance under WHAT.*

## THE MIND

The next column is the MIND, which is the first of the three reasons <u>why</u> we struggle. The mind holds our beliefs. What we believe affects how we feel and causes what we do! *"As a man thinks, so he is"*. (Proverbs 23:7) To understand why we struggle, we must examine the beliefs in our mind about God, ourselves, others and life. This is often the most difficult part of the inventory to complete.

Most of us are not aware of what our specific thoughts are. They have been unconsciously developed by us over a lifetime, based on the beliefs in our culture, the values of our parents, or created as the result of our experiences. **Because we have lived with a sin nature and separated from God, the beliefs in our mind may not be consistent with God's truth.**

To identify the thoughts and beliefs of your mind, refer to the worksheet at the end of this lesson that lists <u>COMMON THOUGHTS AND BELIEFS</u>. Ask yourself these questions, and then write your beliefs under MIND:

    a. What did I think or believe to be true about God, myself, others or life as result of this struggle?
    b. What outcome did I imagine as the result of the experience with WHO and WHAT?

Now, referring back to Eve's inventory, consider the beliefs in her mind. While we can't really know for sure what she was thinking, we can make some assumptions based upon the actions she took. Considering the questions above, the following is an inventory of the possible thoughts and beliefs in Eve's mind.

- She did not believe the truth of God's words. Because He told her 'no', she thought He didn't want her to be happy.
- She believed what the Serpent said. Even though it conflicted with what God said, it was in agreement with what she saw and wanted.
- Finally, she believed she could depend on herself to figure out what to do. She imagined that if she ate the fruit, she would be like God. She made a decision to eat the fruit!

*Now, looking at your inventory, ask yourself the questions listed previously to help you identify the thoughts or beliefs in your mind. Write down your thoughts/beliefs in the next column entitled MIND. Resist the urge to ignore thoughts you believe you shouldn't have, or to judge your thoughts. Read through the list of **COMMON THOUGHTS AND BELIEFS** and list what the Holy Spirit reveals to you.*

Congratulations! You have now completed Part One of your inventory! But don't pack up to leave the Oasis of Examination yet! You will continue in the examination process next week to finish the remaining columns.

# COMMON THOUGHTS AND BELIEFS

## *About Myself*

I should control, fix, or rescue other people.

If only I were ___ then ___.

I know what is best for me and others.

I don't deserve anything good.

I should be who others want me to be.

What I think, feel or need does not matter.

I am alone. Nobody cares about me.

I can get it right if I try harder.

I should get my life together.

Everything depends on me.

I am unlovable, a failure, hopeless.

I don't matter. I am a mistake.

I hate myself because _____.

I never get "it" right.

I earn acceptance and love by my performance, others' approval or more possessions.

I can be happy if others are happy.

I am entitled to have what I want.

If I only had _____ I would be happy.

I must avoid pain at all cost.

I need more money or power to feel secure.

I am better than other people.

I should try harder, know better, and do more.

If I _____ then _____.

## *About Others*

Other people hurt or reject me.

Other people are not trustworthy.

Other people know what is best for me.

Other people should not have to suffer.

Other people need me to help them.

Other people should meet my needs for love, support or approval.

Other people are the reason I am like this.

Other people should obey me and/or God.

Other people should try harder.

Other people are better than me.

If they _____ then I _____.

## *About God*

God doesn't care about me.

God has abandoned me.

God asks more than I can give or do.

God doesn't love me.

If God _____ then I or they _____.

God punishes me.

God doesn't have my best interests at heart.

God doesn't understand me.

God doesn't hear me.

God doesn't talk to me.

God wants me to suffer.

God is not trustworthy.

God is never happy with me.

God doesn't help me.

## *About Life*

Life should be fair.

Life should be as I would have it.

The purpose of life is to get what I want.

The purpose of life is _____

My life should have no _____

My life should include _____

- Be Honest
- Do Not Judge Your Responses
- Resist the Urge to Protect Others

Date: _____

# MY INVENTORY

| WHO | WHAT | WHY | | | |
|---|---|---|---|---|---|
| | | MIND | HEART | | |
| | | | DESIRES | FEELINGS | ACTIONS |
| The Person with whom you struggle | The incident or cause of your struggle | List the beliefs and thoughts you have about life, yourself, others, God or the future as a result of this struggle | List your unmet desire as a result of this struggle | List how you feel about this struggle | Describe what you did as a result of this struggle because of your beliefs, desires and feelings |
| | | | | | |
| | | | | | |
| | | | | | |
| | | | | | |
| | | | | | |
| | | | | | |

*God loves you... just as you are, not as you think you should be. There is nothing you have done that ever changes His love for you.*

Steps Into God's Grace        Lesson 12-At the Oasis: Inventory-Part One

- Be Honest
- Do Not Judge Your Responses
- Resist the Urge to Protect Others

Date: _____

# EVE'S INVENTORY

| WHO | WHAT | WHY — MIND | WHY — HEART — DESIRES | WHY — HEART — FEELINGS | ACTIONS |
|---|---|---|---|---|---|
| The Person with whom you struggle | The incident or cause of your struggle | List the beliefs and thoughts you have about life, yourself, others, God or the future as a result of this struggle | List your unmet desire as a result of this struggle | List how you feel about this struggle | Describe what you did as a result of this struggle to take control, cover, hide or blame. |
| God | She hears do not eat from that tree. God set a limit for her. | 1. God told me "no". 2. Do not believe His words are true. 3. God doesn't want my happiness. | 1. Want to set my own limits. 2. Want to establish my own identity. 3. Desire to eat apple. | 1. Angry—don't like being denied. 2. Afraid I will not have what want. 3. Envious of God's identity | 1. Ignored God's word. 2. Rejected God's authority. |
| Serpent | He told her if she ate from tree her eyes would be opened and she would be like God. | 1. I can be like God. 2. God doesn't care about me. 3. Believe Serpent's words true. 4. I can have what I want. | 1. Want to be like God: to have God's identity-control, power. 2. Want what I want, when I want, how I want. | 1. Hopeful (expectant joy) that there is a way for me to have what I want: identity of God. | 1. Chose to believe Serpent because his words offered her an identity she desired. |
| Self | She is confused about what to do. She sees fruit that is pleasing, but has two conflicting sets of information. | 1. I can figure out what is right. 2. I can be like God. 3. Imagine being like God. 4. I can reach out and eat-and have what I want. | 1. Want to be wise and limitless like God. 2. Want to provide what seems best to me for me. 3. Don't want anything to get in way of my purpose/plan to be like God. | 1. Hopeful (expectant joy) that I have power to obtain what want. | 1. Depended on self to get what she desired 2. Took Control: used hand to reach out and eat. 3. Covered nakedness with fig leaf. 4. Hid from God in trees. 5. Blamed Serpent. |

*God loves you… just as you are, not as you think you should be. There is nothing you have done that ever changes His love for you.*

Steps Into God's Grace     Lesson 12-At the Oasis: Inventory-Part One

# STEPS INTO GOD'S GRACE

## LESSON 13: At the Oasis: Inventory-Part 2

At this point in your journey you may see that self-examination is hard and at times emotionally painful. You may feel overwhelmed with the awareness of the limitations of your humanity and the effects of sin in your life. You may even want to give up and stop meeting with the Holy Spirit, leave the Oasis of Examination and go back to living as you once did.

I too had many fears and concerns during my first examination. I was afraid God would be disgusted with me when He saw what I really desired and felt. I thought He might abandon me as everyone else in my life had. Was I too broken for Him to love me or restore me? Would He condemn me for my actions?

Now I know the blessing that truth brings, and I have found the Holy Spirit to be very gentle. I was not probed endlessly and painfully. I was not harmed or shamed. I was not rejected. I was loved in a way I had never been loved before. What I learned during my time at the Oasis is that I had nothing to fear. I was safe in my heavenly Father's arms. He always knew the truth about me and He loved me just as I am. While His purpose was to gently reveal truth to me, He only revealed as much as I could handle at that moment. So I encourage you to go to your next appointment. You will not find judgment and condemnation, but grace and mercy. You will find healing water for your parched soul.

***What fears do you have, or what encouragement can you offer to others to continue with examination?***

_____

_____

## YOUR THIRD DIVINE APPOINTMENT

Now the Holy Spirit beckons you to your third appointment at the Oasis of Examination. He waits for you to invite Him into the precious territory of your heart, to join you as you examine your desires and feelings. *"The Lord doesn't see things the way you see them. People judge by outward appearance, but the Lord looks at the heart."* (1 Samuel 16:7 NLT) Then He will help you examine your actions which are caused by your feelings and desires. *Even a child is known by his acts, whether (or not) what he does is pure or right.* (Proverbs 20:11 AMP) An inventory of your heart and actions will help you see why you struggle and have problems in your relationships.

***What will the Holy Spirit examine in your next appointment? Why?***

_____

_____

# INVENTORY: PART TWO

Now, through the inventory of our heart's desires and feelings and our actions, the Holy Spirit will reveal the specific ways sin manifests itself in our lives, which is another reason why we struggle! Before you continue, place the MY INVENTORY and EVE'S INVENTORY forms from Lesson 12 in front of you.

# HEART'S DESIRES

The next column on your inventory is DESIRES. You studied the God-given desires of the heart in Lesson 11, and this would be a good time to review that part of Lesson 11. Now you will learn how these desires have been corrupted by sin and separation from God. *"The strong desire of man's heart is evil and wicked from his youth."* (Genesis 8:21 AMP)

Like most humans, you have been confused about your identity, and didn't know your purpose. You created an identity based on what you do and questioned who to trust and what was true. To help you identify the specific desires in your heart, ask yourself the following questions as you consider each WHO on your inventory.

1. What identity did you expect the WHO to provide? Would your relationship with this person help you be known as a good mother, husband, sister, daughter, son, worker, Christian or friend? Would it help you be known as good, successful, special, important or valuable?
2. What did you expect this person to <u>provide</u> for you? Did you want food, shelter, or rest? Did you want knowledge, comfort or help? Did you desire respect or affirmation?
3. What <u>protection</u> did you expect this person to provide for you? Did you desire physical or emotional safety, or did they interfere with your ability to feel safe physically, emotionally or financially?
4. Did you desire <u>love</u> from this person? Did you want acceptance, approval, sympathy, companionship, or intimacy? You desire love when you seek companionship, a relationship, marriage, or children. You desire love when you crave empathy, sympathy, compassion or friendship. You often desire love when you seek kind words, gifts, or attention.
5. What goal or <u>purpose</u> was obstructed by this person or circumstance?

Once again, to help with your understanding of the inventory of DESIRES, return to Eve. After identifying who she struggled with, the facts of her struggle and the beliefs in her mind, we consider the possible desires in her heart. Based on her actions and the questions listed above, we discern that she desired to have the power to set her own limits. She wanted to establish her own identity–to be like God, not just human. She desired to determine what seemed right in her eyes and provide for her own needs for food. She trusted herself more than God to fulfill her plan and purpose. (Refer to EVE'S INVENTORY)

*Now, using the inventory forms on which you have completed WHO, WHAT, MIND, ask yourself the questions listed above to help you identify the desires of your heart, which were thwarted by this person or circumstance. Be as honest as possible. List them under DESIRES.*

## HEART'S FEELINGS

Now, move to the next column of your inventory labeled FEELINGS. This part of your inventory will expose your feelings as the result of your unmet desires. Bringing your feelings into the light will reveal the truth and begin God's process to heal you.

Sin caused us to have selfish, self-centered desires. These desires for what we want, when we want it, and how we want it cause us to feel anger or sadness when they are not fulfilled. Our heart now seeks fulfillment of its own selfish desires; it demands its own way, keeps records of wrongs, and gives up more frequently than it endures. We have passion for the wrong things, not God's purpose for our life. We trade joy for happiness, which is dependent on outward circumstances, not inward peace. What was intended to bring us to repentance and dependence on God now causes us shame and regret, which motivates us to fight for what may not be ours to have. (Please refer to Lesson 1 and Lesson 11 to remind you of the different feelings and their purposes)

Eve may have had many different feelings as she encountered God and the Serpent in the Garden: anger because she was told she could not have what she wanted; fear that she would not get what she wanted; hope because she believed knew a way to get what she wanted, and because she believed she was powerful enough to get it. Feelings of shame, guilt and fear engulfed her when she acted out of her desires and ate the forbidden fruit.

*Now let's return to your inventory. For each WHO and WHAT you listed, review the first two columns under MIND and DESIRES. Then allow yourself to feel, maybe for the first time, any feelings that arise and list them under FEELINGS. Refer to the list of <u>COMMON FEELINGS</u> at the end of this Lesson to aid in your response.*

## ACTIONS

So far, we have identified what we believe, our desires, and how we feel. Now we are ready to complete the last column of our inventory. We will list the ways we responded to these thoughts, desires and feelings under ACTIONS. The picture of why we struggle will now become clearer.

Our actions are not random responses to our circumstances; they are ways of living determined by minds and hearts that have been corrupted by sin. Our actions, which are learned behaviors that have been practiced and perfected by us over time, fall into four main categories:

1. **TAKE CONTROL** We depend on our efforts to take action which will force life to be the way we want it.

2. **COVER** We create or project an image of perfection for ourselves and the life we desire. The image helps us disguise our weaknesses, imperfection, or motives. It conceals our limits and mistakes.
3. **HIDE** We avoid God's presence, look away from God's truth or deny our true thoughts and feelings to protect ourselves. We keep secrets.
4. **BLAME** We shift responsibility for a fault, wrong, choice or consequence to someone or something besides our self by condemning someone or something else.

To help you identify the actions you take to make your life work, refer to the list of COMMON ACTIONS at the end of this lesson and ask yourself the following questions.

a) What did you do to take control to fix the problem or get what you wanted?
b) What did you do to avoid the struggle or the consequences of your choices?
c) What did you do to try to stop your pain or the pain of others?
d) What did you do to satisfy your desire for identity, provision, protection, love or purpose?
e) How did you cover your true identity, weakness or failure?
f) How or where did you hide? What secrets did you keep?
g) How did you defend your beliefs or protect yourself or others?
h) Who did you blame? What excuses did you make?

Consider the actions of Eve. **Since the beginning of humanity, man's ways have been the same: take control, hide, cover and blame.** Believing she could be like God by eating the fruit, she took control by ignoring God's Word and rejecting God's authority. She chose to believe the Serpent and eat the fruit in an attempt to achieve the identity she desired. She covered her nakedness with a fig leaf, hid from God in the trees and blamed the Serpent.

*Now let's turn to your inventory and consider your ACTIONS. In the last column write what you did to take control, hide, cover or blame during each struggle you listed. Refer to the list of COMMON ACTIONS at the end of this lesson.*

Congratulations. You have now completed the examination process. You should now have a better understanding of the examination process and will continue to work with your sponsor to do a comprehensive inventory.

# COMMON FEELINGS

## *Fear*
I feel fear of rejection.
I feel fear of abandonment.
I feel fear of pain.
I feel fear of making a mistake.
I feel fear of people.
I feel fear my children won't be okay.
I feel fear of an unknown future.
I feel fear of getting old.
I feel fear of not being able to take care of myself.
I feel fear I will disappoint people.
I feel fear of failure.
I feel fear of not being a good mother/wife/sister/Christian, etc.

## *Anger*
I feel furious.
I feel irritated.
I feel offended.
I feel frustrated.
I feel resentful.

## *Pain*
I feel brokenhearted.
I feel lonely.
I feel sad.
I feel depressed.
I feel miserable.
I feel self-pity.

## *Shame*
I feel ashamed of_____.
I feel shame that I make mistakes or fail.
I feel worthless.
I feel unlovable.
I feel ashamed that I doubt God.
I feel like I don't matter.
I feel humiliated.
I feel left out/not important.
I feel disgraced.
I feel shame that I don't know what to do.

## *Guilt*
I feel guilty that I _____.
I feel at fault for getting a divorce.
I feel guilty that I don't serve enough.
I feel guilty that I can't/didn't _____.
I feel guilty that I hurt others.

## *Love*
I love/worship my image (physical appearance, reputation, success)
I love/worship others.
I adore my clothes/house/car/things.
I feel no love.
I love others' good opinion of me.
I feel devoted to my children, husband.
I love/worship_____
I feel love when _____

## *Joy*
_____ gives me joy.
I feel happy when _____
I feel happy when others are happy.
I feel happy when life goes as I want.
I feel happy when others approve of me.
I feel happy when I get what I want.
I feel joy when I (or others) follow the rules.
I feel no joy.
I feel happy when I perform better/have more than others.

## *Passion*
I feel passionate about the environment.
I feel passionate about politics.
I feel enthusiastic about good books.
I feel passionate about food.
I feel obsessed about having a happy family.
I feel obsessed about having successful children.
I feel passion for physical or emotional intimacy.
I feel obsessed about being respected.
I am obsessed with being loved.
I feel passionate about doing the right thing.
I am obsessed with others doing the right thing.
I feel driven for success or perfection.
I feel passionate about having a happy life.

# COMMON ACTIONS/ WAYS

## *I USE MY THOUGHTS*

Ignore my or others needs

Seek to understand, figure out

Deny pain or discomfort

Deny my feelings or instincts

Believe what you say about me

Judge myself better than others

Judge others better than myself.

Refuse to accept reality

Constantly think about problems

Ignore my values

Trust my thoughts

Minimize the truth

Exaggerate the truth

Justify my fantasy

Doubt God's Word or promises

Create a plan

Focus on my past

Focus on what is wrong, ignore good or vice versa

Assume I know what others want

Assume others know what I want

Don't value my talents and gifts

## *I USE/DON'T USE MY WORDS*

Lie or tell half the truth

Use humor to avoid or minimize my feelings

Control with angry words

Tell others what to do

Control with words of encouragement

Shame or belittle others

Share too much with others

## *I USE/DON'T USE MY WORDS*

Ridicule others

Gossip

Rationalize others' behavior

Condemn failures or weakness

Verbally abuse

Use guilt messages to persuade

Give directions or take charge

Yell or scream at others

Use sarcasm to express feelings

Tell you what you want to hear

Complain to everyone for sympathy

Don't reveal all my true thoughts and feelings.

Avoid confrontation or procrastinate

Say "yes" when I mean "no"

Keep silent

Don't ask for what I want or need

Laugh to avoid honesty

Talk negatively about myself

Twist God's Word

Expose others' weakness

Don't verbalize my limitations

Always say I am sorry

Minimize my value and worth

Don't use my abilities/talents

## *I USE/DON'T USE MY HANDS/FEET*

Stay busy to escape problems

Seek to rescue or save others

### *I USE/DON'T USE MY HANDS/FEET*

Addicted to helping or being nice

Intentionally under perform

Compulsively put others' needs first

Run away when hurt or angry

Physically abuse people or things

Follow the rules or "the shoulds"

Do not leave when being hurt

Pretend to be like others

### *I USE/DON'T USE MY ABILITIES*

Fix problem

Perform for or take what I want

Seek perfection

Seek to be in control

Establish my authority

Keep trying harder

Work excessively

### *I USE THINGS*

Food for comfort

Sleep for comfort

Drink or use drugs for comfort

Use medication for comfort

Use _____ for comfort

Acquire more things

Hide in books, phone, TV, computer, etc.

Use money, job, or power

Give things for attention, approval, love

### *I USE OR ABUSE MYSELF OR ALLOW OTHERS TO USE ME*

Always put myself last

Seek to perfect my outward appearance or behavior

Give up on my wants and needs

Self-rejection and abandonment

Force myself to be perfect

Condemn myself

Volunteer to be a victim

Do nothing when I am hurt or angry

Physically abuse myself

Over eat/under eat

Over-exercise/under exercise

Allow others to push me past my limits

Accept that which is unacceptable

Depend on myself for everything, even if I am not responsible

Judge self harshly

Allow others to tell me who I should be, how I should act

Pity myself

### *I USE OR ABUSE OTHER PEOPLE*

Use sex for comfort

People please for love or attention

Focus on others to escape my problems

Seek others' attention/affection so I matter

Depend on someone to care for me

Substitute sex for love

Reject people who disagree with me

Use people for sense of identity, value

Avoid people

Use relationship to avoid self

Withdraw from others when hurt

Blame others

Compare myself to others

Try to make others happy so I am happy

Others' opinion determines my value.

# STEPS INTO GOD'S GRACE

## LESSON 14: Blessing at the Oasis

We followed the Holy Spirit into the wilderness, and He led us to the Oasis of Examination. Here God provided what seemed to be bitter water and inadequate food. We may have complained and often resisted attending the meetings appointed for us. Yet, as we allowed the Holy Spirit to examine our minds, hearts and actions, He slowly fed us knowledge of the truth. For those who chose to drink and eat of God's provision, we found the water to be sweet and the food abundant to meet our daily needs. This manna God so graciously supplied was the knowledge of the truth of how God created us and the effects of sin in our lives.

When I met with the Holy Spirit in the Oasis of Examination and received the blessing of truth about myself, I came to know more of the truth of who God is as well. I came to know His faithfulness, gentleness and compassion as He examined my heart without condemnation. As I became willing to receive His provision of truth, I experienced His love. I experienced His patience as He waited for me to choose to show up for my appointments.

My experience at the Oasis of Examination was not what I expected. In some ways it was harder, as I looked at things I did not want to see. But the shared, deep personal experience of those with me on the journey made it a joyful process. Most of all, the Holy Spirit fulfilled the deep longing in my heart to know the truth about myself and how much God loves me. This made His love for me more real and increased my ability to believe and trust Him more.

***What, if any, experience did you have of God's love, provision or protection for you as His child at the Oasis of Examination?***

_____

_____

***What truths have you come to know and understand about the character of God?***

_____

_____

***How has this affected your ability to believe and trust God?***

_____

_____

## DO NOT FORGET

*"And you shall (earnestly) remember all the way which the Lord your God led you...in the wilderness, to humble you and to prove you, to know what was in your (mind and) heart...He*

*allowed you to hunger and fed you with manna, which you did not know nor did your fathers know…"* (Deuteronomy 8:2-3 AMP)

After our time at the Oasis of Examination, we will follow a practice the Israelites performed during their journey in the wilderness. We will create a memorial to the significant event that took place here. Because we are human and are prone to forget, our personal memorial will serve to remind us of the manna (heavenly food) God provided for us.

*"Thus says the Lord, the Redeemer of Israel, …the Lord, Who is faithful, the Holy One of Israel, Who has chosen you,…in an acceptable and favorable time, I have heard and answered you, and in a day of salvation I have helped you; and I will preserve you…saying to those who are bound, Come forth, and to those who are in darkness, Show yourselves… They will not hunger or thirst, neither will mirage (mislead) or scorching wind or sun smite them; for He Who has mercy on them will lead them, and by springs of water will He guide them."* (Isaiah 49:7-10 AMP)

God used our time at the Oasis of Examination to open my eyes to the truth of my condition. The blessing of truth I received was:

> My eyes are drawn away by many "shiny things" in the world which distract me from my God-given purpose. I have a tendency to believe the words of man more than those of God. I believe I am right, and I have the responsibility for everything and everyone, including their happiness! I cling to the idol of my thinking to determine what is right. I insist on doing things in my own way and by self-effort without God's direction. I create my identity in my job or my children. I rely on other people to be my source of security and love. My mouth is often silent in an effort to project agreement or to avoid rejection and humiliation. If I speak, my words contain more condemnation and criticism than forgiveness and acceptance. I use my feet to help me run away from painful situations or perform to achieve approval. I have a tendency to hide in the comfort of my home or busyness to avoid my feelings of pain and sadness. I put up walls in my relationships to keep others from knowing my weaknesses and failures. Then I blame others for my suffering and cover the truth with a mask of "nice". All my desperate attempts to satisfy my desires cause me to live in darkness and despair.

***Now it is time for you to summarize the blessing of truth you received at the Oasis of Examination. This will help you remember the truth that was brought to light as God's blessing for you while you were here.***

***To help you describe the truth of how God created <u>you</u> and how sin and separation from God have specifically affected <u>your</u> life, I have prepared the attached worksheets. Fill in your name at the top of this worksheet, and then answer the questions based on what was revealed <u>only</u> in your inventory.***

DATE _____

## CURRENT CONDITION OF _____, BELOVED CHILD OF GOD

## MIND

1. WHAT DO I BELIEVE ABOUT GOD? _____

2. WHAT DO I BELIEVE ABOUT MYSELF? _____

3. WHAT DO I BELIEVE ABOUT OTHERS? _____

4. WHAT DO I BELIEVE ABOUT LIFE? _____

5. I HAVE A TENDANCY TO BELIEVE WHAT I SEE OR HEAR FROM THESE SOURCES MORE THAN GOD's TRUTH: _____

## HEART: DESIRES

1. WHAT DO I DESIRE OR DEPEND UPON FOR MY <u>IDENTITY</u>? _____

2. WHAT DO I CLING TO FOR MY <u>PROTECTION</u>? _____

3. WHAT DO I DESIRE OR DEPEND UPON FOR THE <u>PROVISION</u> OF MY NEEDS? _____

4. WHAT DO I DESIRE OR DEPEND UPON TO MEET MY NEED FOR <u>LOVE</u>? _____

5. WHAT DO I DESIRE TO HAVE AS MY <u>PURPOSE</u>? _____

6. WHAT DO I HAVE A TENDANCY TO DEPEND ON TO MAKE MY LIFE WORK? (PEOPLE, THINGS)
_____
_____

7. WHAT DESIRES ARE STRONG MOTIVATORS IN MY LIFE?
_____
_____

# HEART: FEELINGS

1. WHAT DO I FEEL SHAME FOR? _____
2. WHAT DO I FEEL GUILTY ABOUT? _____
3. WHAT OR WHO DO I FEAR? _____
4. WHAT AM I IN PAIN ABOUT? _____
5. WHAT AM I ANGRY ABOUT? _____
6. I HAVE A TENDANCY TO BECOME DISCOURAGED OR DEPRESSED WHEN: _____
7. I HAVE A TENDANCY TO BECOME AFRAID WHEN: _____
8. I HAVE A TENDANCY TO BECOME ANGRY OR PRIDEFUL WHEN: _____
9. WHAT FEELINGS TEND TO DOMINATE MY HEART AND CONTROL MY ACTIONS MOST? _____

# ACTIONS

1. WHAT ACTIONS DO I HAVE TENDANCY TO TAKE WHEN I DON'T GET MY WAY? _____
2. WHAT ACTIONS DO I HAVE A TENDANCY TO TAKE WHEN SAD OR IN PAIN? _____
3. WHAT DO I DO WHEN IF FEEL GUILTY OR ASHAMED? _____
4. HOW DO I RESPOND WHEN AFRAID? _____
5. IN ORDER TO AVOID RESPONSIBILITY, WHAT DO I DO TO HIDE, COVER OR BLAME? _____
6. WHEN CONFRONTED BY A PROBLEM, I HAVE A TENDANCY TO IGNORE GOD AND TAKE THE FOLLOWING ACTIONS TO GET WHAT I DESIRE: _____

This truth did not come from your mind or your wisdom. This knowledge was not known to you before your times in the Oasis of Examination. You were blind, but now can see yourself as God sees you. You know your limits and your wounds. You have been given insight to see the truth of your condition: what you believe, what you desire, and how you live. Without condemnation or judgment, God revealed your many characteristics of a child of man. You have now completed Step 4. But thankfully, this is just the fourth step of your 12 Step journey. God does not intend to leave you in this condition. He has only brought the truth to light so that His process of healing can begin.

# STEPS INTO GOD'S GRACE

## LESSON 15: The Mountain of Confession-Part One

We have completed our time at the Oasis of Examination, and it is now time to leave. The Holy Spirit is beckoning us, *"Come let's climb God's mountain, to the House of God...He will show us the way He works so we can live the way we're made."* (Isaiah 2:3 MSG) We will travel to the Mountain of Confession where you will come out of hiding and learn how to live unafraid and without shame.

Our hearts are heavy with the new awareness of the effects of sin in our lives, and we are concerned about what lies ahead. Some of us, fearful of stories of God's anger and judgment, want to turn back; however, we take courage from our fellow companions. We pray for the strength to climb the mountain and meet with God.

***What is your initial reaction to the Holy Spirit's call for you to climb the Mountain of Confession? What encourages you to continue?***

_____
_____

## STEP 5: COMING OUT OF HIDING

Paul, in his letter to the Romans, sends a message of hope to all God's beloved children. He assures us that we are not alone. All have sinned and fallen short of the glory of God. All people suppress the truth, do not honor God, are futile in their thinking and trust in idols. All people blame and judge others harshly and despise God's kindness. But because of God's Rescue Plan through Christ and God's inheritance for us as His children, we do not have to live with the burden of our past sins! God has provided a way for our hearts and minds to be cleansed and purified of sin.

*"My little children, I am writing these things to you so that you may not sin. But if anyone does sin, we have an advocate with the Father, Jesus Christ the righteous; and he is the atoning sacrifice for our sins...God is light...if we walk in the light as he himself is in the light, we have fellowship with one another, and the blood of Jesus his Son cleans us from all sin. If we say we have no sin, we deceive ourselves, and the truth is not in us. If we confess our sins, he who is faithful and just will forgive us our sins and cleanse us from all unrighteousness."* (John 2:1-2 and 1 John 1:7-9)

Here at the Mountain of Confession, we learn God's Way for us to deal with our sin. We no longer need to hide ourselves as our parents Adam and Eve did. God invites us to come and talk it over with Him. We will take **Step 5:** ***Admit to God, to ourselves and to another human being the exact nature of our wrongs.***

The Mountain of Confession is the place where we overcome our denial and pride. As God's Sons and Daughters, we will practice rigorous honesty with God, self and others! *We're not keeping secrets, we're telling them. We're not hiding things; we're bringing everything out into the open.* (Luke 8:17 MSG) **Confession breaks the bondage of our pride and frees us of the burden of our sins. It allows us to live humbly, unafraid and without shame.**

*You're blessed when you're content with who you are – no more, no less.* (Matthew 5:5 MSG)

***As a child of God, we no longer hide our sins, we practice confession. Why?***

_____

_____

_____

## **THE EXACT NATURE OF OUR WRONGS**

At the Mountain of Confession, we begin by identifying the exact nature of our wrongs. Then we will confess these wrongs to God, ourselves and others. During our time at the Oasis of Examination, we learned much about how God created us and how sin and separation from God has negatively impacted our mind, heart and actions. We listed our wrong beliefs, desires and actions. Now it is time to clarify the exact nature of our wrongs.

Over the years, through many examinations, and with the help of scripture and my sponsor, I have received much insight into the exact nature of my wrongs. What follows is what I have come to know about myself.

> Many of my strongly held beliefs are nothing more than illusions and lies that distorted my perception of the world and others. They kept me from knowing reality and held me in bondage. I lived as a prisoner to my wrong beliefs, selfish desires and feelings of shame, pain, fear and guilt.

> As the result of sin, my motives were selfish and self-centered. Unable to accept my limits and failures, I lived in fear because I saw my circumstances only in light of my limited power and understanding. My unwillingness to acknowledge my human limitations caused me shame. Instead of depending on God to meet my needs, I substituted money, power or other people for my security. My dependence on these idols caused me to live in fear of conflict, rejection, abandonment or failure, and enslaved me to things that always failed me.

> My actions were merely my self-efforts to hide my failures, protect my weaknesses and satisfy my selfish, insatiable desires. I ignored God and believed He would not accept me. I chose to put myself into areas that were not my concern, taking responsibility for others' lives, then falling victim under the burden I chose to carry. In my failure to accept the reality of my limits and needs, I rebelled and sought to create my own

identity. I ignored the spiritual, physical and emotional needs of my body and harmed myself by under-eating, not exercising, or over medicating yourself. My obsessive thinking to find a "better way" exhausted me. To act as if I could control such things, and then beat myself up because of my failures, was foolishness.

I used the gift of helping, given to me by God, for my own purposes. I made others dependent on me by providing for their needs so I could feel good about myself, or worse, create an identity for myself. My gift became my addiction. I made an idol of this behavior. I used people to meet my needs for identity, provision, protection and love, expecting them to affirm and love me in return. Moreover, I used relationships to avoid my pain or emptiness without God.

*It is time for you to identify the exact nature of your wrongs. To help you with this process, refer to your inventory and your completed worksheet from Lesson 14 as you answer the following questions.*

1. *Read Jeremiah 7:8. How did you ignore or deny God's truth of:*

    a. *The limits of your humanity?*
    _____
    _____

    b. *The true character of God?*
    _____
    _____

    c. *The authority of Christ?* _____
    _____

2. *Read Isaiah 42:20. How were you futile and godless in your thinking because of the lies you believed about God, yourself, others, or life?*
    _____
    _____
    _____
    _____
    _____

3. *Read Jeremiah 17:9. How did you not honor God and His will, but glorified yourself by:*

    a. *Creating your own identity?*
    _____
    _____

    b. *Using your abilities or giftedness to meet your needs or desires?*
    _____
    _____

    c. *Worshiping people, power, or possessions instead of God?*
    _____
    _____

    d. *Depending on people, power or possessions for your comfort, protection and provision?*
    _____
    _____

    e. *Developing your own plan and purpose for your life?*
    _____
    _____

4. *Read Isaiah 30:1. How did you take control, hide, cover, and blame to get what you wanted instead of trusting God?*
_____
_____

5. *How did your wrong thoughts, desires, feelings, and actions harm you or others?* _____
_____

*As you consider your answers to the previous questions, what is most surprising to you about the exact nature of your wrongs?*
_____
_____
_____

## TALKING IT OVER WITH GOD

*"Come now, let us reason together," says the Lord. "Though your sins are like scarlet, they will be white as snow..."* (Isaiah 1:18 NIV) God waits with a heart full of love and acceptance–never condemnation--for you to come to Him. He waits to give you wisdom, teach you what is true, and provide the healing and forgiveness you need. Because you are God's Child, you have nothing to fear. Christ has paid the price for all your sin. He redeemed you, and *"there is now no condemnation (no adjudging guilty of wrong) for those who are in Christ Jesus..."* (Romans 8:1 AMP)

God loves you just as you are. Nothing you confess to God is a surprise, nor will it ever change His love for you. But through confession you will experience the blessings of God's compassionate grace and mercy. Confession will allow you to apprehend your God-given inheritance: cleansing and freedom that leads to transformation!

*I acknowledged my sin to you, and my iniquity I did not hide. I said I will confess my transgressions to the Lord (continually unfolding the past till all is told) –then You forgave me the guilt and iniquity of my sin. (Psalm 32:5 AMP)*

**What blessings do God's children receive when they confess?**

_____

_____

*It is time for you to acknowledge your sin and expose your iniquity to your Father. Maybe it's a whisper or maybe a loud cry that escapes your lips as you climb into His arms and say "Here I am, Daddy… this is what I believe, feel, desire and have done."*

*Consider your answers above and your inventory. Slowly begin to open yourself to God.*

1. *As honestly as you can, talk face-to-face with God about the exact nature of your wrongs. Confess your wrong beliefs, sinful desires and harmful actions.*
2. *Now reflect on Romans 8:1-2, Hebrews 13:5, 1 John 1:7-9, Jeremiah 30:3 and Jeremiah 31:13-14.*
   *What new wisdom, freedom or healing did you receive as you considered these words from God for you?*

   _____

   _____

   _____

3. *How do you feel after meeting with God at the Mountain of Confession?*

   _____

   _____

   _____

# STEPS INTO GOD'S GRACE

# LESSON 16: The Mountain of Confession-Part One

For many of us, meeting with God at the top of the Mountain of Confession was not at all what we expected! We thought God wouldn't love us if He really knew us. We thought He wouldn't want us for His Son or Daughter. But what we found was a Father whose love was greater than our failures and mistakes. He told us we could never do anything that would change His love for us. We did not have to perform for Him. We did not have to hide from Him. We were safe in His arms!

While we may want to stay at this place of such mercy and grace, the Holy Spirit indicates that it is time to take the long road back to the base of the mountain. Before we leave, however, He charges us to remember that God is our Father who loves us greatly and Christ is our Savior and King. We should not forget this: we will always tend to doubt His Word, believe what we see and hear more than His Truth, or be controlled by our desires and feelings more than His will. This is when we must remember God's promises: *"The days are coming, when I will release you from captivity,...and I will break (the oppressor's) yoke from your neck, and I will burst your bonds; and strangers will no more make slaves of you...For I am with you...I will restore health to you and I will heal your wounds."* (Jeremiah 30:3-17AMP) *"I will turn your mourning into joy and will comfort you and make you rejoice after your sorrow. ...You will be satisfied with My goodness."* (Jeremiah 31:13-14 AMP)

With these encouraging words in our hearts, we continue on our journey to the base of the Mountain of Confession. There we will continue on the Way by first admitting the exact nature of our wrong to ourselves and then another person who we trust.

***How do you feel about confessing the truth to yourself? Another person? Why?***

_____

_____

## STEP 5: TALKING IT OVER WITH YOURSELF

*It is now time to admit the truth to yourself. With the help of your inventory and your answers to the questions in Lesson 15, complete the following:*

1. **MY WRONG BELIEFS**

    *"But one thing I do know, that whereas I was blind before, now I see."* (John 9:25 AMP)

*To confess the ways you were blind to the truth, list, and then read aloud, the lies you believed about yourself, God, others and life. I wrongly believed:*

_____
_____
_____
_____

2. **MY WRONG DESIRES**

In the next part of your confession to yourself, you will name the wrong desires and feelings in your heart. To help you with a better understanding of your heart, I have included below a description of the seven deadly sins all humans exhibit, paraphrased from *Drop the Rock* by Bill Pittman and Todd Weber (pp. 40-53).

Pride: Believing myself to be more than human, I think I know best and am responsible for everything and everyone. False pride is settling for inferiority or being less than human.

Envy: We fear we won't get "the good things" and resent when others do.

Gluttony: We have sloppy habits of taking care of this temple of the spirit. We lack balance in what provides us with energy, health, strength and endurance.

Sloth: Spiritual procrastination in all areas of our life. Procrastination is not living one day at a time; not doing what we are meant to do today.

Covetousness: We have to possess what others have. We must own and keep and grasp and hold tight all that we can.

Lust: We confuse sex with love, or lust with desire, or sex with being intimate; thus experiencing remorse and guilt from self-motivated sexual actions.

Anger: Anger is poison. It is emotional drunkenness that causes us to act out of uncontrollable rage when we perceive our will is being thwarted.

*Confess a time when you experienced these sinful desires/feelings in your heart.*

*Pride:* _____

*Envy:* _____

*Gluttony:* _____

*Sloth:* _____

*Covetousness:* _____

*Lust:* _____

*Anger:* _____

*First list, and then say aloud to yourself, the wrong desires and feelings of your heart. I did not live in accordance with God's will, but wrongly desired:* _____
_____
_____

_____

3. **MY WRONG ACTIONS**

   Finally, your confession to yourself includes naming the actions you took as the result of your wrong beliefs and wrong desires.

   *List, and then read aloud to yourself, the ways you used your God-given freedom to substitute your efforts for God's power. I ignored God's authority and ways, and I took control of my life and the lives of others through my wrong actions of:*
   _____
   _____
   _____
   _____

   *List, and then read aloud, the harms you caused by taking control, covering, blaming or hiding. I harmed myself or others by my wrong actions of:*
   _____
   _____
   _____

*How do you feel after making a confession of the exact nature of your wrongs to yourself? Why?* _____
_____

## STEP 5: TALKING IT OVER WITH ANOTHER PERSON

It is time now to talk with another person about ourselves. Consider each of your new friends who seemed to share similar struggles. Then choose someone trustworthy who has been on this journey before and with whom you feel safe to share your sins, hurts and failures. Make an appointment to share your inventory with them.

*"Confess to one another therefore your faults (your slips, your false steps, your offenses, your sins) and pray (also) for one another, that you may be healed and restored (to a spiritual tone of mind and heart)."* (James 5:16 AMP)

**With whom have you chosen to share your inventory? _____**

**Do you think this person is safe and trustworthy? Why?**

_____

The Apostle Paul provided an example of confession when he admitted His struggles to other believers. He said, *"I've spent a long time in sin's prison…I decide one way then act another, doing things I despise….I know the law but I cannot keep it…I need help…I don't have what it takes…I can't do it…I decide to do good, but don't…My decisions don't result in actions…Something has gone wrong deep within me…Parts of me covertly rebel."* (Romans 7:14-23 MSG)

*"I do admit that I have fears, that when I come, you'll disappoint me and I'll disappoint you, and in frustration with each other everything will fall to pieces—quarrels, jealousy, flaring tempers, taking sides, angry words, vicious rumors, swelled heads and general bedlam."* (2 Corinthians 12:20 MSG)

Paul's confession was an honest expression of his failures. He was willing to take a risk to express his fears of disappointing others, being rejected or being condemned. That is what we will do in our confession to another.

Brennan Manning writes in the *Ragamuffin Gospel*, *"There is no growth in Christ Jesus without some difficulty and fumbling. If we are going to keep on growing, we must keep on risking failure throughout our lives. In spite of the fact that Christianity speaks of the cross, redemption and sin, we're unwilling to admit failure in our lives. Why? Partly because it is human nature's defense mechanisms against its own inadequacies. But even more so, it's because of the successful image our culture demands of us."*

**What fears or concerns do you have about confession to another person?**

_____

_____

In the *Codependent's Guide to the 12 Steps* (pg. 87), Melody Beattie writes, *"To begin that process (of soul-level change), it is imperative that we unearth, release, get rid of, and be done with shame, fear, guilt, secrets, and anything else inside us that bothers us, causes us to feel less than, weighted down by, burdened by, and bad about ourselves. The way to do that is by opening our mouths and getting it out. It is a simple but effective way to begin healing ourselves. We simply tell the truth about ourselves to ourselves, to another person, and to God in an attitude of self-responsibility, acceptance and forgiveness."*

*What makes confession worth the risk of rejection?*

## **OVERCOME OUR BATTLE WITH PRIDE**

Maybe like me, you do not want to humble yourself and be honest with another person about what you learned at the Oasis of Examination! In fact, there seems to be something operating in each of us that is desperate to cover our inadequacies and failures. When I read this poem by Beth Moore, I knew what it was: Pride.

<u>My Name is Pride</u>
by
Beth Moore

My name is Pride. I am a cheater.
I cheat you of your God-given destiny…
   because you demand your own way.
I cheat you of contentment…
   because you "deserve better than this."
I cheat you of knowledge…
   because you already know it all.
I cheat you of healing…
   because you are too full of you to forgive.
I cheat you of holiness…
   because you refuse to admit when you are wrong.
I cheat you of vision…
   because you'd rather look in the mirror than out a window.
I cheat you of genuine friendship…
   because nobody's going to know the real you.
I cheat you of love…
   because real romance demands sacrifice.
I cheat you of greatness in heaven…
   because you refuse to wash another's feet on earth.
I cheat you of God's glory…
   because I convinced you to seek your own.
My name is Pride. I am a cheater.
You like me because you think I'm always looking out for you.
Untrue.
I'm looking to make a fool of you. God has so much for you, I admit, but don't worry…If you stick with me you'll never know.

*After reading this poem, what revelation have you had about how pride has cheated you?*

_____

_____

*How does this affect your willingness to confess your sins to another person you trust? Why?*

_____

_____

A Step 5 confession is always done face-to-face between one humbled, contrite heart to another. It may take more than one meeting to share our confession. **The first part of the process begins when we push through our fear and shame to open our mouths and reveal our true beliefs, desires, feelings and ways from our written inventory.** It will be uncomfortable at first; however, this new way of living provides release from feelings of shame and guilt that control us. It is important to remember that if we truly want to be free, the one thing we most desire to hide is probably the very thing that is most important for us to reveal.

**In the second part of the process, we ask for more truth.** Because we have learned that we are blind to the self-deceptive ways of our sinful nature, we ask the other person to give us a better perspective on our beliefs, desires, feelings, or actions. We welcome this blessing of truth, which will enable us to grow emotionally and spiritually.

When I completed my first confession with another person, I experienced "being heard" for the first time. I received compassion or empathy for my wounds. I heard, "I know how you feel, I have felt the same way", or "I have done that too." As a result, I began to know that I was not alone and that my behaviors were not that different from others. I also received more understanding and insight about my beliefs, desires and my actions. For the first time, I experienced someone who revealed the truth of who they were and accepted me just as I was. Finally, I experienced freedom from the debilitating shame and guilt of my past! This was God's Blessing for me at the Mountain of Confession!

*Meet with someone you trust this week and share <u>at least one</u> struggle, WHO, WHAT and WHY, from your inventory. Then describe what you experienced before, during and after your confession (Step 5) with another person.*

_____

_____

_____

## <u>INTO THE LIGHT OF GOD'S GRACE</u>

It is a mystery how or why God's Way of confession works, but it is enough for us to know that this is His way for us as His children to be cleansed, freed and healed. All we do is obey. We may not understand now, but after we have obeyed, we will understand.

*"As soon as you set your foot on the Way, I'll show you my salvation."* (Psalm 50:23 MSG)

It did not happen right away, but over time, after my confession, I began to experience a sense of "lightness" or freedom I did not have before. I no longer felt isolated, worse than everyone else, or alone. I began to welcome my limits that I had denied, ignored or disowned. Finally, I realized I was becoming more whole as I embraced my humanity, my strengths as well as my weaknesses.

**What blessings did you receive by coming out of hiding and practicing the Way of Confession?**

_____
_____
_____

## PRAY FOR EACH OTHER

Finally, confession is always followed by prayer. In James 5:16, we are instructed to *"confess our sins to one another and pray for each other that we may be healed."* We encourage and support each other in our struggles through prayer. Together we thank God that He provided the Way for us to be free of our guilt and shame. We ask that He will give each of us the help we need to live in the Truth or reality He has so graciously revealed to us. We pray that we may each be healed!

**What do you want others to specifically pray for you?**

_____
_____
_____

*You have now practiced the Step 5 process for this part of your journey. Continue to practice this step with your sponsor as needed.*

**How has the practice of Confession helped you come out of hiding?**

_____
_____
_____
_____

# STEPS INTO GOD'S GRACE

## LESSON 17: The Valley of Repentance

The Holy Spirit bedded us down by quiet pools in the Oasis of Examination and guided us to the Mountain of Confession. He gently, but directly, made us aware of our blind eyes, deaf ears and lame feet. We saw how we lived as prisoners, enslaved to lies, false idols, fear, shame, hurt and despair. We came out of hiding and admitted the truth to ourselves, another person and God.

While we now know that the needs of our soul can never be met by the world, other people or even ourselves, it seems, however, that our journey is not over. No sooner have we caught our breath, the Holy Spirit directs us to travel to the valley below. We pack our bags and head down the rocky trail with deep sorrow in our heart. We have the companionship of our fellow travelers, but we are alone with our thoughts. We have heard rumors that we are headed to the Valley of Repentance--a place where many sad people dwell.

*How do you feel as you approach the Valley of Repentance?*

_____
_____

## STEP 6: THE WAY OF REPENTANCE: LIVE BY FAITH

Repentance is not only seeing our wrongs and the pain it causes, but also becoming willing to follow the Way of Faith. This is **Step 6:** *Were entirely ready to have God remove all these defects of character.* Our repentance indicates that we are entirely ready to have God change us. We do not have to believe lies, or depend on others' approval and our own efforts to make life work! God can change us! God's Kingdom is here!

In in *Carry on, Warrior,* Glennon Doyle Melton writes, *Repentance is the magical moment when a sliver of light finds its way into a place of darkness in my heart, and I'm able to see clearly how my jerkiness is keeping me from peace and joy in a specific area of my life.* (p. 85):

*What does it repentance mean to you, and how is this different from what you thought repentance meant?*

_____
_____

*What might motivate you to take Step 6?*

_____
_____
_____

If we are honest, even with the awareness of our brokenness, most of us don't want to change. But then, we don't want to stay the same either. We really just want others to change so we can be okay as we are. It is then that the Holy Spirit reminds us:

*"The people who sat (dwelt, enveloped) in darkness have seen a great Light, and for those who sat in the land and shadow of death Light has dawned. From that time Jesus began to preach, crying out, "Repent (change your mind for the better, heartily amend your ways, with abhorrence of your past sins), for the kingdom of heaven is at hand..."* (Matthew 4:16, 17 AMP)

*"Repent (have a change of mind which issues in regret for past sins and in change of conduct for the better) and believe (trust in and rely on, and adhere to) the good news (the Gospel)".* (Mark 1:15 AMP)

Now knowing the truth of my limited humanity and sin nature, I heard Jesus words in a new way. He was crying out directly to me. I did not have to live any longer enslaved to my sin nature and weighed down by the burdens of my past sin! I did not have to hide in a prison of sorrow and regret for my limitations and failures. Jesus brought a message of hope: Change your mind, make a radical turn from your silly ways of self-effort and self-preservation, believe the Good News and depend on God! God's Rescue Plan was His good news for me <u>today</u>! My salvation did not come through my self-effort; it was a free gift of God. I understood Jesus is my only hope for deliverance or restoration of my mind and heart. My part was to repent, not just work harder to change my selfish or controlling behaviors, but be willing to live by faith in God's work to change me!

***Now that you are aware of your true condition, what hope does Jesus proclaim for you today, and how might this motivate you to take Step 6?***

_____
_____
_____

## **OUR DESPERATE CRY**

Just because others choose to continue to live in an illusion, believing they are in control, thinking they know best and calling evil "good" and good "evil", this is no life for us. God wants us to come to Him for help!

*"If you get rid of unfair practices, quit blaming victims, quit gossiping about other people's sin...your lives will begin to glow in the darkness, your shadowed lives will be bathed in sunlight. I will always show you where to go. I'll give you a full life in the emptiest of places—firm muscles, strong bones. You'll be like a well-watered garden, a gurgling spring that never runs dry. You'll use the old rubble of past lives to build anew, rebuild the foundations from out of your past."* (Isaiah 58:9-12 MSG)

Are you willing to return to the Truth? Are you willing to quit taking control and blaming others? Are you willing to turn from your self-centered life to a God-centered life? Repentance is how you put your faith in action! If you are willing to repent, God will give you a new life!

*"For indeed we have had the glad tidings (Gospel of God) proclaimed to us just as the Israelites of old did; but the message they heard did not benefit them, because it was not mixed with faith (with leaning of the entire personality on God in absolute trust and confidence in His power, wisdom and goodness) by those who heard it."* (Hebrews 4:2 AMP)

**How do you feel about Jesus call to you to "Repent"?**
_____
_____

**What may be blocking your willingness to repent?**
_____
_____

# LET GO

The purpose for us at the Valley of Repentance is to become entirely willing to have God change us. We do this by letting go of our self-effort, wrong beliefs, false idols and wrong actions, and turning to faith in God. *"Let us strip off every weight that slows us down, especially the sin that so easily hinders our progress..."* (Hebrews 12:1 NLT)

Rick Warren wrote in *Daily Hope: A weight is anything that slows you down. It could be a relationship, a job, an activity, or a sport. It doesn't have to be a bad thing. A weight can be a good thing, but if you get too many good things in your life, you're going to collapse because you don't have time for all of them. You need to learn to say "no" to grow. God doesn't expect you to do everything. A weight can also be an unreasonable expectation that comes from peer pressure of the need to please someone, or it can be a memory. You might be stuck in the past, holding on to a happiness or hurt. The problem is that you can't live in the past or even in the future; you can only live in the now. Trying to do anything else will weigh you down. Whatever the weight is, if it isn't working in your life, if it's dragging you down, you need to let it go.*

**What good things may you need to turn from, fast from or let go of in order to progress on your journey?**
_____
_____
_____

If you are like me, you may want change, but are afraid to fail! I was afraid to let go of all the things that made me feel comfortable, safe and loved. What would I do, or who would I be, if I did not have my hopes and dreams or my ministry or my work? How could I live without the approval of others? Who would I be if everything didn't depend on me? I acknowledged my fears, as one by one, I considered the things I need to let go of:

    My belief that everything depends on me
    My expectations, hopes and dreams for a perfect life
    My need to please others and receive their approval
    My ministry or my job as my identity
    My family members' health and welfare
    My manipulative ways I used to control other people or circumstances

***Consider your inventory. Which of your wrong beliefs, desires, feelings, or actions are you willing to let go of right now?***

_____

_____

***What fears do you have about what it would mean for you to let this go?***

_____

_____

Repentance is not easy. In fact, it is much easier to choose regret and despair over change. This is why so many people choose to stay in the Valley of Repentance instead of just visiting there. I felt deep sorrow for my sins, and with God's help, I wanted to be willing to change my mind and actions. I wanted to give up my identity as a child of man. I wanted to live as a child of God. Yet, the knowledge that this change would require me to turn from self-dependence to God-dependence seemed overwhelming. I was firmly attached to my beliefs, desires and ways. I could not imagine a life without them. But I heard the Holy Spirit's words, *"Therefore, also now, says the Lord,* **turn and keep on coming to Me with all your heart, with fasting, with weeping, and with mourning** *(until every hindrance is removed and the broken fellowship is restored). Rend your hearts and not your garments and return to the Lord..."* (Joel 2:12-13 AMP)

I knew I wept for my sin, but I did not understand what it meant to come to the Lord with fasting. I thought fasting was only abstaining from physical food, but I realized that the fast God called me to was **a fast that included abstaining from my old wrong beliefs, desires and actions.** I was to turn to God, weeping for my sin, and willing to fast from negative thinking, false beliefs, harmful speaking or attempts to control outcomes. My fast was to be a "letting go" of self-reliance, hiding from God, blaming others, playing God and carrying burdens I was never intended to carry. This was the difference between regret and repentance.

***What do you believe God is asking you to fast from, or let go of, as you come weeping and return to the Lord in repentance?***

_____

_____

Change is hard. The process of letting go may cause pain. We may experience irritability or sadness as we let go of our dreams. We may feel uncomfortable as we let go of familiar, controlling behaviors. We may experience fear of an uncertain future, or fear of the unknown. Feelings of emptiness may overtake us as we lay down our image of "nice", "good", "perfect", or "wise". Others may get angry at our changes. We may question who we are if we stop being who we think we should be, or who others expect us to be. We may question what we will do with ourselves when we are not consumed with maintaining our image or defending our behaviors. But when we let go of the weight of our past, we are free to move into a new life of trusting God.

***What do you question or fear will happen to you if you let go?***

_____

_____

Fenelon wrote in *Let God* (p. 46): *When we come to these valley experiences, when we are deprived of faith and assurance, there is only one thing to do. We must go straight on through the valley, walking with the Shepherd just as we did before we entered that valley. As we go through, let us deal with any sin which the Lord reveals to us, still walking in the light He gives…completely dependent on His mercy….*

***Are you ready to move from the Valley of Repentance, or do you still struggle to believe and trust God? Why?***

_____

_____

***What hope would you offer someone who is struggling to let go?***

_____

_____

## LIVE BY FAITH

We are not alone. We are God's children. We do not have to live with a heart that does not work as God intended. We can let go of dependence on our mind and efforts to make life work and choose to live by faith in God. He will start over to re-create everything in our lives! By faith, we inherit His promises of transformation, healing and peace. *"I have been crucified with Christ; it is no longer I who live, but Christ who lives in me; and the life I now live in the body I live by faith in (by adherence to and reliance on and complete trust in) the Son of God, Who loved me and gave Himself up for me."* (Galatians 2:20 AMP)

I could not make myself perfect or overcome my sin nature on my own. Only by letting go of my self-effort and idols could I then choose to live by faith and have room for God to work in my life. The more I was willing to surrender and abandon myself to complete reliance on God, the further along the sacred Holy Road I could travel. Step 6 is turning away from my self-effort to make my life work, and turning to God, trusting Him to change me. The main difference between how to live as a child of man, compared to life as a child of God, is faith! *"Now faith is the assurance of things we hope for, being the proof of things we do not see and the conviction of their reality (faith perceiving as real fact what is not revealed to the senses)."* (Hebrews 11:1 AMP)

Living by faith includes:

1. A daily letting go of my wrong beliefs, desires and ways
2. Trusting God to do for me what I am not able to do for myself
3. Looking for God to work in the midst of every struggle
4. Allowing His Spirit to lead me, instead of relying on my natural impulses

**What have you come to understand about how to live as a child of God as you spent time in the Valley of Repentance?**

_____
_____
_____
_____

*This assignment will help you identify and then let go of (REPENT) of your wrong beliefs, desires, and actions in order to live by faith as a CHILD OF MAN. You will use the BE TRANSFORMED worksheet at the end of the lesson for this assignment. I have provided a completed sample at the end of the lesson to help guide you in this process.*

1. *Choose one struggle from your MY INVENTORY, which includes a <u>wrong belief</u> that you are willing to let go.*

2. *Copy the WHO, WHAT, WHY from the struggle you chose above onto the <u>"CHILD OF MAN" section of the BE TRANSFORMED worksheet at the end of this lesson.</u>*

3. *Stop. Next week you will complete the "CHILD OF GOD" section at the bottom of the form.*

Date: _____

# BE TRANSFORMED

| WHO | WHAT | WHY | | | ACTIONS |
|---|---|---|---|---|---|
| | | HEART | | | |
| | | MIND | DESIRES | FEELINGS | |
| | | **CHILD OF MAN** | | | |
| My Son | Unable to keep a job, he wants my help with financial needs for food and rent | Everything depends on me. | I desire to do things perfectly. | I am afraid of rejection. | I pretend to have answers. |
| | | My son will reject me if I do not help. | I desire to be accepted and loved. | I afraid that he will be homeless. | I hide my fear. |
| | | I should protect my son from suffering. God doesn't care about my problem. Life is unfair. | I desire to help and protect everyone. | | I think obsessively for ways to fix the problem. |
| | | | | | I use his happiness to meet my need for love. |
| | | | | | I always help, even if not asked. |
| | | **CHILD OF GOD** | | | |
| | | I am not God. I am His child.( John 1:12) | I desire to know God and His will. | I feel loved and accepted by God. | I am honest with my son about my financial limits. |
| | | God is in control. (1 Chronicles 29:11-12) | I desire to trust God with my son's well-being. | I feel freedom to be a limited human. | I confess my fear of rejection to God. |
| | | I do not know if my son will reject me. | I desire relationships that are unconditional. | I feel some fear of loss of relationship. | I seek God's guidance for me. |
| | | My son is responsible for his life before God. It is not my job to do for him what he can do for himself. I can trust God. | | | I wait, pray and trust God to provide what is necessary for my son. |

Date: _____

| WHO | WHAT | BE TRANSFORMED ||||
|---|---|---|---|---|---|
| | | MIND | WHY HEART || ACTIONS |
| | | | DESIRES | FEELINGS | |
| | | **CHILD OF MAN** |||||
| | | | | | |
| | | **CHILD OF GOD** |||||
| | | | | | |

Steps Into God's Grace      Lesson 17-The Valley of Repentance

# STEPS INTO GOD'S GRACE

## LESSON 18: The Pool of Transformation

Leaving the Valley of Repentance, we are called by the Holy Spirit to set out once again on a new path. While it looks dangerous, our faith in God motivates us forward. We have hope in our hearts. *"For we, through the Holy Spirit's help, by faith anticipate and wait for the blessing and good which our righteousness and right standing with God (our conformity to His will in purpose, thought, and action) causes us to hope."* (Galatians 5:5 AMP)

The time passes quickly, and we soon find ourselves beside a cool, clear pool where we think the Holy Spirit has led us here to wash our bodies, especially behind our ears and between our toes! But He has something entirely different in mind. He intends to cleanse our minds and hearts, which are so dirty that we are barely human at all. He knows that when the mind believes truth, hearts will be motivated by God's will, and actions will be in accordance with God's ways. At the Pool of Transformation, God's children are restored to the people God created them to be! *"May God himself, the God who makes everything holy and whole, make you holy and whole, put you together—spirit, soul and body—and keep you fit for the coming of...Jesus Christ."* (1 Thess. 5:23-24 MSG)

How long will you remain by the pool believing you can provide the healing you need? How long will you live in fear of letting go of your beliefs, hopes, or ways? Will you let God cleanse you and make you a holy temple? *"Dear friends, let's make a clean break with everything that defiles or distract us, both within and without. Let's make our entire lives fit and holy temples for the worship of God."* (2 Corinthians 7:1 MSG)

**Are you willing to cooperate with God so you can be cleansed at the Pool of Transformation? Why?**

_____
_____

## STEP 7: CHANGE YOUR MIND

What we believe is one of the greatest obstacles to our having an abundant life! Because what we believe affects what we feel and causes what we do, any change to our heart and actions must begin with changes to the beliefs in our mind! *"Do not be conformed to this world, (fashioned after and adapted to its external, superficial customs), but be transformed (changed) by the (entire) renewal of your mind (by its new ideals and its new attitude), so that you may prove what is the good and acceptable and perfect will of God."* (Romans 12:1-2 AMP)

**What can you expect to happen at the Pool of Transformation?**

_____
_____

It is not always our physical wandering that enslaves us. Often the wanderings of our minds carry us to places we need not go--into the past or the future. All our thoughts of "if only" generate feelings of guilt or shame. All our thoughts of "what if" generate fear. Both keep us from living in the present, where God's grace is sufficient. We need to learn to discipline our mind to live within the limits God set for us! Choosing to believe truth and to stay in the present are acts of faith—faith that God has our past and our future in His hands. All is in God's control, not ours. We ask God to accomplish in us what we have been unable to do for ourselves. We take **Step 7:** ***We humbly ask God to remove our shortcomings.***

To renew our minds, *"We refute arguments and theories and reasonings and every proud and lofty thing that sets itself up against the (true) knowledge of God; and we lead every thought and purpose away captive to the obedience of Christ."* (2 Corinthians 10:5 AMP) To take every thought captive:

1. We test each thought to determine if it is true. We take each belief listed on our inventory and ask, "Is it true that it all depends on me? Is it true that others will reject me if I do not do as they ask? Is it true that things will never work out or get worse unless I intervene? It is true that they <u>always</u> act that way? Is it true that_____?"
2. Then we compare the imaginings and assigned meanings of our minds to the truth! *"There is nothing like the written Word of God for showing you the way to salvation through faith in Christ Jesus. Every part of Scripture is God-breathed and useful one way or another—showing us truth, exposing our rebellion, correcting our mistakes, training us to live God's way."* (2 Timothy 3:14-17 MSG) We look for God's truth. Talk it over with our sponsor and seek other trusted companions for counsel. We wait on God to reveal His truth to us in His timing.
3. If our belief proves to be false, we replace it with the truth.
4. As we cooperate with the Spirit's power and God's Word, our mind will be renewed (changed) and we will be transformed. We will believe God's thoughts, desire God's will, and our ways will be God's ways.

***How do you participate with God at the Pool of Transformation?***

_____

_____

Transformation is a mysterious and deliberate spiritual process by which the Holy Spirit renews our minds. It is a process we do not control. The Holy Spirit directs the process and will complete it over our entire lifetime. We can ask to have just one belief removed at a time. The process is sometimes painful, but as we cooperate with the Spirit, we receive a new mind that believes the truth. We will no longer be confused about what is true. As our thoughts become God's thoughts, we will have peace of mind! With a new mind, come new actions. Gradually, we are born of the Spirit into an entirely new way of life!

*"And God will wipe the tears from every face. He'll remove every sign of disgrace from His people, wherever they are. Yes! God says so!"* (Isaiah 25:8 MSG)

***What blessing did you receive as a child of God at the Pool of Transformation?***

# HUMBLY ASK HIM TO RENEW OUR MINDS

At the Pool of Transformation, we ask God to *"Send out your light and your truth and let them guide me."* (Ps 43:3 NLT) To do this, we will substitute God's truth for the lies we believe about Him, about ourselves, and about how life should work. We won't always do it perfectly, but the process will become easier with each attempt, Old patterns of thinking will be renewed and transformed. Our trust in God will grow. Our actions and lives will be changed! The Holy Spirit now reminds us, *"I have no greater joy than this, to hear that my children are living their lives in the Truth."* (3 John 4 AMP) *"Steep yourself in God-reality, God-initiative and God-provisions."* (Matthew 6:33 MSG)

<u>Complete the remainder of the BE TRANSFORMED worksheet you started in Lesson 17.</u> *Refer to the sample provided in Lesson 17 for guidance.*

1. <u>**TEST YOUR BELIEF.**</u> *Test the beliefs which you listed at the top of the worksheet under CHILD OF MAN: MIND. Seek the truth about yourself, God, others and life. Read God's Word. Discuss your beliefs with the Holy Spirit and your sponsor.*

2. <u>**BE RENEWED IN YOUR MIND**</u>: *Substitute the truth for your beliefs. Write the truth and scripture references under CHILD OF GOD: MIND.*

3. <u>**BE TRANSFORMED**</u> *Continue across the worksheet. Write down your desires and feelings as you consider this new truth. Pray for God to change your heart if necessary. Read God's Word and ask the Holy Spirit to direct your actions as CHILD OF GOD. List the actions you should take and scripture references. (See last page of this lesson for suggestions for new actions.)*

*Practice these new beliefs and ways of living in a circumstance this week. What were the results?*

_____
_____
_____
_____

<u>You have now practiced Step 7.</u> *How did God renew your mind and transformed your heart and actions through this process?*

_____
_____
_____
_____

# ACTIONS OF A ...

## CHILD OF MAN

1. Prideful
2. Stubborn
3. Dishonest
4. Cover (Deny)
5. Worry
6. Judgmental
7. Arrogant
8. Procrastinate
9. Hide
10. Take Control
11. Gossip
12. Enable
13. Busy
14. Take Revenge
15. Live By My Will
16. Live By My Mind
17. Blame

## CHILD OF GOD

1. Humble (1 Peter 5:5, 6; Prov. 11:2)
2. Willing (1 Chronicles 28:9)
3. Honest (Romans 12:17; Prov. 12:5)
4. Examine And Repent (Lam. 3:40)
5. Trust (Prov. 3:5; 1 Peter 5:7)
6. Compassionate
7. Teachable (Prov. 4:11-13; Prov. 10:17)
8. Prompt (Prov. 12:27)
9. Confess (James 5:16)
10. Seek God (Matt. 6:33)
11. Trustworthy (1 Peter 3:10)
12. Love (1 Corinthians 13:4-8)
13. Be Still (Psalm 46:10; Prov. 14:30)
14. Pray (1 Peter 3:9)
15. Live For What God Wills (1 Pet. 2:16, 4:2)
16. Live By The Spirit (1 Peter 4:6)
17. Forgive

# STEPS INTO GOD'S GRACE

## LESSON 19: The River of Forgiveness

Our journey so far has been difficult, but it is also proving to be life-changing. With minds that are being renewed, we can now comprehend the vast difference between our beliefs and God's truth. Our experiences of God's supernatural freedom and cleansing are helping us come to believe in the magnitude of God's love and His power for us! But even after all we have experienced, our hearts are still broken and aching!

Immediately, we hear the Holy Spirit, "Arise, go to the River of Forgiveness. There God will teach you about the power of forgiveness." Once again we travel to a new place where we hope God will do for us what we have been unable to do all our lives—heal our broken hearts.

*Where are you going now, and why?*
___

For most of my life, I never understood the power of forgiveness. Now I know that forgiveness is the pardon, or extension of grace, which when offered to someone who has caused harm, releases the resentment and bitterness in hardened hearts! The healing balm of forgiveness heals the shame and guilt of the past that is keeping our hearts from working as God intended. **Forgiveness is the only way to experience lasting healing, health, and freedom from the damage of sin in our relationships with others. Receiving and offering forgiveness will heal more of our problems than any other measure we can take.**

*What is forgiveness, and what does it do?*
___
___
___

*Do you want to be free from shame and guilt from the past?* ___

## STEP 8: GOD'S HEALING PROCESS

Christ settled our broken relationship with God by forgiving us. In the same way, our relationships with others can be healed as we offer and receive forgiveness. To cooperate with God's healing process, we take **Step 8:** *Made a list of all persons we had harmed and became willing to make amends to them all.* We will actively seek to repair the damage we caused in our relationships by making amends. We will admit our wrongs and ask for forgiveness.

*The old life is gone; a new life burgeons! Look at it! All this comes from the God who settled the relationship between us and Him and then **called us to settle our relationships with each other**.* (2 Corinthians 5:16-18 MSG) *All things are from God, Who through Jesus Christ reconciled us* *to Himself (received us into favor, brought us into harmony with Himself) and gave us the* ***ministry of reconciliation.*** (2 Corinthians 5:18 AMP)

As children of God, living in His Kingdom, our new way of life is to live with a ministry of reconciliation! We are to live with a focus on people we have hurt and people who have hurt us, not our outward appearance or achievements. We are to be God's vessels of grace in the world. We forgive as we have been forgiven. We acknowledge the hurt and pain we endured as the result of others' offenses toward us, and then forgive. We seek forgiveness from others for the harm we have caused. While we cannot undo what was done, our steps to offer or ask for forgiveness from ourselves or others can help heal the wounds. As far as it depends on us, we eagerly seek to settle our relations with God, self and others.

***Did you know you have been given a ministry of reconciliation?*** _____

***What does it look like to live with a ministry of reconciliation?***
_____
_____

## MAKE A LIST OF ALL PERSONS WE HAVE HARMED

Our old way of blaming others is not beneficial for us as God's child. Our past actions wounded others and ourselves, as well. We are ready to get honest and stop blaming others for the harms we caused. We work with our sponsors to identify <u>our part</u> in the struggles, and then make a list of those we have wronged and the specific ways we offended or hurt God, self and others. Finally, we become willing to seek healing in these relationships by making amends. *I will walk in my house with a blameless heart.* (Psalm 101:2 NIV)

### MY RELATIONSHIP WITH GOD

The truth for all of us is this: We ignored God's sovereignty and our identity as His beloved children. Our thoughts are not his thoughts and our ways are not His ways. We took control, covered our sin nature, hid from God and blamed Him for our struggles. We did not receive His love nor did we respect His ways. We did not love Him in return.

How we must have saddened God and His Son and grieved His Holy Spirit. In effect, we nailed Jesus' hands and feet so they could not help us and rejected His thoughts in favor of our own. We quenched the Holy Spirit's guidance and distrusted the reality of our Father's goodness and faithfulness. We resisted everything that did not fit into our plans. Thankfully, the Holy Spirit reminds us: God was neither disappointed nor surprised by our behavior. His heart felt sorrow over the lack of an intimate relationship with us and the harm we caused our self and others.

*"And they shall look (earnestly) upon Me whom they have pierced, and they shall mourn for Him as one mourns for his only son… (each with an overwhelming individual sorrow over having blindly rejected their unrecognized Messiah)."* (Zechariah 12:10, 14 AMP)

*How have you saddened God by not living in the reality of His identity?*
_____
_____
_____

*Consider your inventory and the exact nature of your wrong in Lesson 15. List the WAYS I HARMED MY RELATIONSHIP WITH GOD:*
_____
_____
_____
_____

## MY RELATIONSHIP WITH MYSELF

Denying the truth of our limited humanity, differences and sin nature, we acted in harmful ways toward ourselves. We repressed our weaknesses or exceeded our limits. Then we blamed ourselves for our struggles.

In *Codependent's Guide to the Twelve Steps,* Melody Beattie writes, *"Allowing ourselves to be lied to and deceived to the point that we no longer listen to or heed our instincts is wrong. Thinking we're bad or wrong for surviving is wrong. Holding other people's issues or inappropriate behaviors against ourselves is wrong....Neglecting ourselves is wrong. Ignoring what we want and need, sometimes to the point that our minds, bodies, and souls rebel by getting sick is wrong. Neglecting or diminishing our gifts and talents is wrong. Being ashamed of ourselves is wrong."*

*Consider your inventory and the exact nature of your wrongs in Lesson 15 and 16. Then list your name and the WAYS I HARMED MYSELF.*
_____
_____
_____
_____
_____

## MY RELATIONSHIP WITH OTHERS

### 1. WAYS I HARMED OTHERS

Because of our wrong beliefs, many of us failed to respect the God-given identity of others and attempted to force them to conform to the image we thought they should have. We may have ignored the reality of their human's limits, differences and sin nature, and expected them to be perfect like God. We were wrong to expect others to be like us. We were wrong to use them to meet our needs for love and acceptance. We were wrong to blame others for our wrong actions, or for not providing for us the life we wanted. We harmed others and others harmed us in the same way. This was not God's plan for human relationships.

*WAYS I HARMED OTHERS: Consider your inventory and the exact nature of your wrongs from Lessons 15 and 16. Talk with your sponsor. Make a list below of the people and ways you harmed others by your wrong judgments, dishonesty, blame, selfish control, or other hurtful actions.*

_____
_____
_____
_____

## 2. WAYS OTHERS HARMED ME

Just as we have harmed others by our wrong beliefs and actions, we have experienced rejection, harm and abuse from others because of their own limited humanity and sin nature. We did not go to God with our wounds, however, but sought to punish and hold others hostage for their wrongs toward us. We stored up memories of wrongdoing and kept bitterness in our hearts. We held on to anger and blamed others for their offenses. (It is important to remember that when considering harms to us as children, we were not to blame. We do not have a part in causing others to abuse us, especially when we were children!)

*Refer to your inventory. Make a list of the harms done to you and the people who cause each harm.*

_____
_____
_____
_____
_____

<u>You have now practiced Step 8.</u> *What did you learn, at the River of Forgiveness, about the power of forgiveness? Where do you see the need for healing balm of forgiveness?*

_____
_____
_____
_____

As the Holy Spirit showed me all the harms in my life, I was deeply grieved. If I wanted to do so much good in life, how could I have caused so much conflict? How could I have resisted reality for so long without knowing what was true? How could I have been so confident in what I believed while being so wrong and causing so much harm? Thankfully, God provided a way for my broken heart to be healed through the power of forgiveness. But we must understand that forgiveness does not mean we forget or condone a behavior. It does mean that we acknowledge the hurt, we ask God to help us forgive those who have hurt us, and we make amends to those we have hurt.

# STEPS INTO GOD'S GRACE

## LESSON 20: The Pathway to Peace-Part One

We do not have to continue to live with broken hearts! God has provided a way for us to be healed. We can seek forgiveness from God, then offer and seek forgiveness from ourselves and others. As we cross the River of Forgiveness, walking on the Pathway to Peace, the Holy Spirit will work in us to replace our heart of stone and give us a new heart. *"For here's what I'm going to do, I'll pour pure water over you and scrub you clean. I'll give you a new heart; Put a new spirit in you. I'll remove the stone heart from your body and replace it with a heart that's God willed, not self-willed. I'll put my Spirit in you and make it possible for you to do what I tell you and live by my commands. …You'll be my people; I'll be your God!"* (Ezekiel 36:25-27 MSG)

God is faithful and His promises are true. It is important to remember, however, that the Pathway to Peace is a slow journey. It takes time to cleanse and heal hearts from all the damage of the past. Forgiveness should never be forced. It is always a Spirit-led process.

## STEP 9: THE WAY OF PEACE

At the River of Forgiveness we will begin walking on the Pathway to Peace. We will take **Step 9:** *Made direct amends to such people wherever possible, except when to do so would injure them or others.* In settling our relationships with God, self and others, our broken hearts we will be healed by the power of forgiveness.

***What is the Pathway to Peace (Step 9)?***

_____

_____

When we make peace, or live with a ministry of reconciliation, we will no longer have to look away in shame from those we hurt or disappointed. We will no longer have to hide or deny the guilt that previously gripped our hearts and pulled us down into pits of despair. We can seek peace. By the power of forgiveness our hearts will be freed from the debilitating feelings and desires that opposed God's will. *The fruit of the Holy Spirit (the work which His presence within accomplishes) is love, joy, peace, patience, kindness, goodness, faithfulness, gentleness, self-control.* (Galatians 5:25 and 23-24 AMP)

In the *Big Book of Alcoholics Anonymous,* Bill W. promises, *"If we are painstaking about this phase of our development we will be amazed before we are half way through. We are going to know a new freedom and a new happiness. We will not regret the past nor wish to shut the door on it. We will comprehend the word serenity and we will know peace. No matter how far down the scale we have gone we will see how our experience can benefit others. That feeling of uselessness and self-pity will disappear. We will lose interest in selfish things and gain interest in our fellows. Self-seeking will slip away. Our whole attitude and outlook upon life will change.*

*Fear of people and of economic insecurity will leave us. We will intuitively know how to handle situations which used to baffle us. We will suddenly realize that God is doing for us what we could not do for ourselves."* (pp. 83, 84)

**What promise do you most look forward to receiving when you take this step? Why?**

_____
_____
_____

## MAKE PEACE WITH GOD

The Holy Spirit calls out to us, *"Search for peace (harmony undisturbedness from fears, agitating passions and moral conflicts) and seek it eagerly. (Do not merely desire peaceful relations with God, with your fellowmen and with yourself, but pursue, go after them!)* (1 Peter 3:11 AMP) Take hold of God's strength and make a complete surrender... **make peace with God! Yes, make peace with God.** He wants you to admit that you have sinned. He wants you to confess your rebellion. He wants you to know He is faithful and just and will forgive your sins and cleanse you from all unrighteousness."

While we may have confessed our sins to God, many of us have not made peace with God. He has offered forgiveness, but we have not accepted His gift. We still hold anger and resentment in our hearts toward Him, or our shame and guilt keeps us from feeling worthy of His free gift. In this step, we will acknowledge the exact nature of the wrongs we hold against Him and seek His forgiveness. Once we receive His forgiveness, our hearts will begin to heal. The shame that has been with us for so long will be released and we will have peace.

Our choice to let go of our stubborn desire to take control and make the rules four ourselves and others is a difficult one. But when we accept the reality of who God is, we can begin to live a life of **peace with God**. By choosing to believe that He knows best, despite what we see, hear or think, we receive **peace of mind**. By choosing to believe He is good and loves us, despite how we feel, we receive **peace of heart**. By confessing our wrongs for the ways we live in conflict with God, we receive forgiveness and **peace with our past**. By choosing to believe He is sovereign, we can stop trying to figure out everything; we can stop taking responsibility for outcomes. This gives us **peace in the present and with the future**.

**How do you feel about making peace with God? Why?**

_____
_____
_____

### *TAKE STEP 9 AND MAKE PEACE WITH GOD*

1. *Take your list of WAYS I HARMED MY RELATIONSHIP WITH GOD from Lesson 19 and find a quiet place by the River of Forgiveness. Pray and read your list to God.*
2. *Then humbly ask for His forgiveness. Imagine Jesus bending down and giving you a drink from the river and saying, "Your faith has made you well. Your sins which are many are forgiven". (Mark 5:34; Luke 7:47)*
3. *Describe your experience.*

_____
_____
_____
_____

*Did settling your relationship with God give you peace? Why?*

_____
_____

*Are there still some barriers to your acceptance of God's forgiveness? Why?*

_____
_____
_____

## MAKE PEACE WITH MYSELF

Once we have settled our relationship with God and received His forgiveness, we begin to see, for the first time, a bridge across the River of Forgiveness, called the Pathway to Peace. God's forgiveness provided a way for us to begin to cross the river and forgive ourselves, and others, as we were forgiven. God knows that while He has forgiven the harms we caused, we have not. At this time, we are each directed to stop on the Pathway to Peace and settle our relationship with ourselves.

*If God has forgiven you, do you still find it difficult to forgive yourself? Why?*

_____
_____

### *TAKE STEP 9 AND MAKE PEACE WITH MYSELF*

1. *Take your list of the WAYS I HARMED MYSELF from Lesson 19.*
2. *On a separate sheet of paper, write a letter to yourself in which you admit your wrongs and ask for forgiveness.*
3. *Respond aloud to the request.*

*Describe how you feel after settling your relationship with yourself.*

_____
_____
_____

(If there are some items on your list that you seem unable to forgive yourself for, talk to your sponsor and ask God for the willingness to forgive yourself.)

As we forgive ourselves, little by little, our hearts will no longer be divided between the one true God and other gods of approval, self-effort, performance, money or possessions. We will live at peace with our limits and differences. We have a process by which we can be freed to love and experience a life of joy and peace with God and ourselves.

*How has taking the steps to make peace with God and yourself healed anger, guilt or shame in your heart?*

_____
_____
_____
_____

# STEPS INTO GOD'S GRACE

## LESSON 21: The Pathway to Peace – Part Two

Lingering at the River of Forgiveness, we have learned that God's Pathway to Peace leads us toward Him and toward our true selves as Children of God. It leads us away from self-hatred, shame and guilt. Now God will lead us to settle our relationships with others, offering forgiveness to those who have harmed us, and seeking forgiveness from those we have harmed. It is simple, but it is not easy.

## MAKE PEACE WITH OTHERS WHO HAVE HARMED US

We make peace with others by first recognizing the reality of their sin nature, their limited humanity, and their differences. We acknowledge how they have failed, hurt or disappointed us, and then we offer them forgiveness. We offer them the same compassion that God offered us. *"Become useful and helpful and kind to one another, tenderhearted (compassionate, understanding, loving-hearted), forgiving one another (readily and freely) as God forgave you."* (Ephesians 4:32 AMP)

***How do you feel about forgiving others as God forgave you? Why?***

_____

_____

While I tried many times in the past to force forgiveness, I now know that I can only humbly offer it to another if I am aware of the depth of my own sin and failure, and the mercy and grace I received. In *Life Together* Dietrich Bonheoffer writes, *"If my sinfulness appears to me to be in any way smaller or less detestable in comparison with the sins of others, I am still not recognizing my sinfulness at all."* (pp. 111-112) And when I do not recognize the depth of my own sin, I cannot have compassion for another.

***Do you still struggle to see others' sin as more detestable than your own? How does this affect your ability to humbly offer forgiveness?***

_____

_____

_____

For years I pursued a false and selfish idea of happiness. I believed lies and harmed others. I rebelled against God, committed adultery and divorced a loving husband. I emotionally abandoned my children and myself. But through the grace of God, I have been forgiven and redeemed and I can humbly look upon others with eyes of compassion, not condemnation. I have great freedom now to forgive others who failed to meet my expectations, validate my efforts, or provide the security or love I desire. *"Freely forgive your brother from your heart his offenses..."* (Matthew 18: 35)

Forgiving does not mean we forget others' harms toward us, but we repent of our hardness of heart toward them. It means we stop putting all our energy into seeking comfort or punishing others for past hurts. We stop holding grudges and feeding on the bitterness. By remembering that others struggle with the same sin disease that we do, we align ourselves with the reality of sin and limitations all humans share, and we seek peace. We offer forgiveness for failures and harms toward us or others whom we love.

Forgiveness releases the resentments and bitterness that poison and enslave us. If we want to be healed and free, we forgive. Since God in His grace has forgiven our transgressions, we are called to forgive others their transgressions against us. Our forgiveness releases them and us from the bondage and poison created by a bitter root of resentment.

***What does forgiveness accomplish in your heart?***

_____
_____
_____

## FORGIVE NOW

1. *Prayerfully consider the names on your list of* **WAYS OTHERS HARMED ME** *Write down the names of those you <u>are willing</u> to forgive now.*

   _____
   _____
   _____

2. *Then say aloud, I forgive _____ for _____.*
3. *Describe any feelings you have as a result of this process.*

   _____
   _____

## FORGIVE LATER

It is important for us recognize, however, that while we may want to be free of our resentments and bitterness, we cannot force ourselves to forgive. Heart-felt forgiveness is only the result of God's internal healing process in us, which may involve our crying or getting angry before we can accept and forgive. Let yourself feel all the pain of those events. Talk it over with your sponsor and God. Ask God to give you a willingness to forgive, so that no root of bitterness will continue to contaminate your heart. Forgiveness can never be forced by us; it may take years to forgive.

***Write the names of people God will have to help you forgive in the future.***

_____
_____

*Write out your prayer to God as it relates to these people and your willingness to forgive them.*

_____
_____
_____

## **PEACE WITH OTHERS I HAVE HARMED**

As we continue on the Pathway to Peace, the Holy Spirit indicates that there is more for us to learn. It is time to make amends, face to face, with those we have harmed. *"As far as it depends on you, live at peace with everyone."* (Romans 12:18 AMP)

The amends process is not to be used to get others to understand us, agree with us or condone our behavior. It is a step of walking in the Way God directs for us; we pursue peace. We choose to clean up our side of the street. We choose to step out in faith to do what God asks of us, because we believe His Way is better than our own. We stop hiding and blaming. We admit our wrongs and ask forgiveness. Then we leave the outcome in God's hands.

*What is the purpose of the making amends with others?*

_____
_____

When I first walked on the Pathway to Peace, I felt panic as I considered my list of those I had harmed. My mind began to race through all the options. How would I know the right words? Would I say everything the right way? What if I made a mistake? How others would respond as I admitted my wrongs? Would I be rejected or humiliated? Maybe I could just put it off until I was more equipped to do this perfectly….

I was fearful, but I no longer wanted to shrink away in shame from those who I harmed. I reminded myself of the Truth that God was with me and would help me. He had provided a way of healing, but I had to choose to walk in the Way. I had to walk through my fears, not around them any longer. But I was not alone! *"So do not fear, for I am with you,; do not be dismayed, for I am your God. I will strengthen you and help you; I will uphold you with my righteous right hand."* (Isaiah 41:10 NIV)

## **SEEK PEACE: NEVER, LATER OR NOW**

We pray for the wisdom to know if we are to make the amends now, sometime later, or never. We cannot make amends when the one we have harmed is no longer alive. Nor should we make amends in cases where it would cause more harm to them or another. In such cases, I have found it helpful to write a letter to this person and then destroy it.

*Do you have someone on your list with whom you will never make face to face amends? Why? As far as it depends on you, how can you make amends?*

_____

_____

Making your amends sometime in the future may be necessary to allow your hurt or angry feelings toward that person to subside before you can go to them with a humble attitude and honest, kind words. Pray for God to soften and heal your heart and then ask Him to provide an opportunity when He knows the time is right.

*With whom might you plan your amends for some time in the future instead of immediately? Why?*

_____

_____

## **WRITE AMENDS, WAIT FOR DIRECTION**

I spent several years in the process of making amends and seeking forgiveness. I started with those I felt led to make amends to right away. I wrote out what I would say to them and then met with my sponsor to discuss the wording. She was helpful to point out where I attempted to justify or rationalize my behavior. Having another's perspective and guidance meant there would be less chance that my amends would cause more harm than good. Then slowly, prayerfully I moved to make amends with everyone on my list. The process was not one I directed, but was one that was being orchestrated for me as God mysteriously provided the words and the opportunities when I was ready.

*How can your sponsor and God help you with the process to write your amends and seek peace?* _____

Some of the hardest amends for me to make were with my children. I had harmed them greatly by choosing to work and be physically or emotionally absent in their lives. Out of my need for significance and value, I robbed them of precious time with a nurturing mother. In addition, I failed to appreciate who God created them to be and spent endless hours trying to coerce them into being who I thought they should be. I admitted my wrongs and committed to change my behaviors toward them by being more available, listening more and speaking less.

*Refer to your list of WAYS I HARMED OTHERS from Lesson 19. Read it over. Find one person you feel led to reconcile with. Now write a letter, using the AMENDS-SAMPLE FORMAT on last page of this lesson. Write the specific ways you tried to control, manipulate or force them into who you thought they should be. Specifically name each of the harmful words or actions you took towards them. Then pray that God will provide the opportunity for you to read your amends to the person and ask for forgiveness.*

*After attempting to write your first amends, what questions do you have about this amends format or the timing of your amends?*

_____
_____
_____

*If you had an opportunity to make the amend this week, or have previously made an amend, what was your experience?*

_____
_____
_____

## **GOD IS IN CHARGE OF OUTCOMES**

We may experience resistance from others when we set out to make amends. They may not be willing to discuss the issue. We can only ask permission to have a conversation and then wait for God to open doors. We never force an amends on someone!

Sometimes our amends process will bring up old wounds in others which may cause more tears or pain. This is normal. We must remember the way for healing is through the pain, not around it. God's way gives us an outlet for healthy expression of our thoughts and feelings and opportunities for our relationships to be healed or restored. Sometimes it will take time for healing to come. Sometimes others will choose not to forgive us. All we can do is trust the process and be obedient to God's direction. We are not responsible for the outcome. Only God is responsible for outcomes.

<u>You have now taken the first steps on the Pathway to Peace (Step 9). Please continue this practice with the guidance of your sponsor and the Holy Spirit until all your amends are completed.</u>

*How has this process healed your heart and helped you stop blaming others?*

_____
_____
_____

You have completed the first two parts of your journey. You have been taught the Truth and learned God's Ways. The last part of your journey begins next week: the Life God's wants you to enjoy.

# AMENDS-SAMPLE FORMAT

First pray and write out your amends, discuss with your sponsor and wait for God to provide the opportunity to make your amends in person whenever possible.

The format should be something like this:

1. <u>Start with an opening statement</u>. "I would like to make amends to you and would appreciate your listening. I will be happy to answer any questions or listen to any comments when I am finished.

2. <u>Name the offense</u> and the circumstance if possible. (Do not include comments which might transfer blame to the other person for your behavior.) Examples:
    a. **It was wrong of me** (out of my need for approval and love) to attempt to control and manipulate you by giving you my answers to your problems.
    b. **It was wrong of me** (out of fear of losing you) to withhold my honest thoughts and feelings and only tell you what I thought you wanted to hear.
    c. **It was wrong of me** (out of a lack of respect for who God created you to be) to try to control you or force you to be who I thought you should be.

3. <u>State the character defect</u>-Examples: I was selfish, dishonest, self-centered, blaming, critical, controlling, abusive, fearful, inconsiderate, etc.

4. <u>State what is true and how you want to change future behavior:</u> Examples:
    a. I want to be honest, encouraging, accepting, kind, etc.
    b. I will seek to not withhold those parts of myself I have been afraid to let you see.
    c. I will seek to have more clear and honest communication.
    d. I want you to feel free to express and explore who God created you to be.
    e. Our relationship is important to me.
    f. You are important to me.
    g. I want to give you time and attention.
    h. I do not want to run away from the problems anymore.
    i. I want to keep my commitments to you.
    j. I want to accept you as you are--a precious child of God. I want to accept our differences and seek to reconcile with you in a manner that honors each other and God in the future.

5. <u>Ask for forgiveness</u>: Examples: Will you forgive me for these actions that caused you pain?

# STEPS INTO GOD'S GRACE

## PART THREE: THE LIFE GOD WANTS ME TO ENJOY

> *The efforts of God are culminating in the gathering of the obedient, disciplined, freely gathered People who know in our day (and will know fully in the days to come) the life and powers of the kingdom of God. This community of People of cross and crown, of courageous action and sacrificial love, who will come to fulfillment beyond time in the formation of the new heaven and new earth teeming with perfectly loving people. Old ways of dominance, alienation, travail, suffering, and morality will give way to life eternal. Worship of self will disappear along with temporal things, giving way utterly to joyous, unending worship of God. (Life with God by Richard J. Foster, p.200)*

# STEPS INTO GOD'S GRACE

## LESSON 22: Hold Fast to the Truth and the Way

We have crossed the River of Forgiveness and completed our time in the wilderness. Over the course of our journey, we have come to know the Truth of who we are and who God is and the Way we are called to live. We experienced a radical internal change in our minds and hearts--the good news of God's Rescue Plan! The Steps we have taken with God have not just cleaned up our past and healed our wounded hearts; they have prepared us to live an abundant life of peace and joy in His presence. We have now arrived in the Land of Promise, where **we will practice holding fast to the Truth, following the Way and living the Life God wants us to enjoy today!**

*"You're kingdom subjects, now live like it. Live out your God-created identity. Live generously and graciously toward others, the way God lives toward you."* (Matthew 5:48) *"Your old life is dead. Your new life, which is your real life—even though invisible to spectators—is with Christ in God. He is your life."* (Colossians 3:3 MSG)

**Where are you now? What is the new Life you are called to live here?**

_____
_____

Now the Holy Spirit speaks. "In the Land of Promise, there will be a proving of what you have learned. You will have opportunities to practice and develop your skills as a child of God and experience the supernatural power of God to act on your behalf. There are many enemies living here. They will war against you with lies and deception that will seek to draw you away from the Truth and cause you to question your identity as God's child. They will attempt to steal what you have received from God in an effort to get you to doubt God's love and His goodness. But *'think of your sufferings as a weaning from that old sinful habit of always expecting to get your own way. There you will be able to live out your days free to pursue what God wants instead of being tyrannized by what you want.'* (1 Peter 4:1-2 MSG). *'Hope in God and wait expectantly for Him, who is your help.'"* (Psalm 43:5 AMP)

**How do you feel as you consider the struggles you will encounter here? Why?**

_____
_____
_____

**What does God promise for you here?**

_____
_____

# STEP 10: PUT ON THE ARMOR OF GOD

At the Oasis of Examination, we learned the value of looking at ourselves and asking God to help us see the ways we lived in opposition to His truth. Later on our journey, we learned to practice confession and forgiveness to acknowledge the truth and heal the harms we caused. Now we are ready to take **Step 10**: ***Continued to take personal inventory and when we were wrong promptly admitted it.*** **The daily practice of continuing to take inventory, confessing wrongs and making amends, provides the spiritual protection we need to maintain pure minds and hearts in the Land of Promise. Step 10 is the process by which we put on the whole armor of God.**

***How does taking Step 10 help us put on the armor of God?***

_____

_____

*"Put on the full armor of God, so that you will be able to stand firm against the schemes of the devil. For our struggle is not against flesh and blood but against the rulers, against the powers, against the world forces of this darkness, against the spiritual forces of wickedness in the heavenly places. Therefore take up the full armor of God, so that you will be able to resist in the evil day, and having done everything to stand firm."* (Ephesians 6:11-13 NASR)

As a child of God, we do not cover ourselves with denial and a false image that is frail and easily defeated. We do not defend ourselves with weak, handmade weapons such as sarcasm, ridicule, condemnation or physical strength. As a soldier in God's army, we put on the **full armor of God** to identify and help us overcome our enemies with divinely powerful weapons. Now, *"for though we walk (live) in the flesh we are not carrying on our warfare according to the flesh and using mere human weapons; for the weapons of our warfare are not physical but they are mighty before God for the overthrow and destruction of strongholds."* (2 Corinthians 10:4)

***How does the armor of God compare to how you have previously protected or defended yourself?***

_____

_____

***Describe a battle you are fighting right now. What you are at risk of losing, or what is challenging your identity or safety, or what is causing you to question God's faithfulness or love for you? (You will refer to this battle when answering the questions that follow.)***

_____

_____

_____

## 1. GIRD YOUR LOINS WITH THE BELT OF TRUTH

*"Stand therefore (hold your ground), having tightened the belt of truth around your loins..."* (Ephesians 6:14 AMP)

We have a tendency to believe lies and make false assumptions based on what we see and hear. This is an area of our lives where we are vulnerable to attack. As a child of God, **we do not trust our limited human understanding, what the world says or what the enemy wants us to believe. We believe God's Word and seek the counsel of the Holy Spirit** to help us separate truth from the finely crafted lies that seek to deceive and enslave us.

***What is the Belt of Truth and why do you need it?***

_____
_____

We put on the Belt of Truth when we discipline our mind from wandering into the past or future. We choose to live within the boundary of today, where we find God's grace. We renew our minds with God's truth. We remember that God is our Father. He has all power and authority. Then, we align ourselves with His truth, which helps us deflect the attacks of lies and deception that can cause confusion, doubt or fear. This is an essential part of our daily, on-going inventory.

*"Set your minds and keep them set on what is above (the higher things), not on the things that are on the earth."* (Colossians 3:2 AMP)

***As you consider the battle you described above, how can you strengthen yourself with the Belt of Truth?***

_____
_____

## 2. PUT ON THE BREASTPLATE OF RIGHTEOUSNESS

*"Put on the breastplate of integrity and of moral rectitude and right standing with God..."* (Ephesians 6:14 AMP)

Because our hearts and the hearts of others are contaminated by sin, we will cause harm or be harmed during this life. We will make mistakes and disappoint others. We will be tempted by lust, jealousy, envy or greed, and sometimes fall into sin. But we do not have to live with hearts heavy with shame, resentment and bitterness. We put on the Breastplate of Righteousness by **drawing close to God and practicing the Ways of Examination, Confession, Repentance and Forgiveness we have been taught.** No more secrets. No more hiding, pretending or blaming. We are honest and take responsibility for our wrong beliefs, feelings and actions. We talk them over with God and another person. We have learned the benefit of not carrying the burden of resentments and bitterness in our hearts. We ask God to cleanse us from any unrighteousness and then make amends to those we have harmed or forgive those who have harmed us. These practices help us maintain a pure heart.

*What is a Breastplate of Righteousness and why do you need it?*

_____

_____

*In your current battle, how can you maintain a pure heart by putting on the Breastplate of Righteousness?*

_____

_____

### 3. SHOD YOUR FEET WITH THE GOSPEL OF PEACE

*"And having shod your feet in preparation (to face the enemy with the firm-footed stability, the promptness, and the readiness produced by the good news) of the Gospel of peace..."* (Ephesians 6:15 AMP)

We have a tendency to forget about our sin nature, our human limitations and God's Rescue Plan for all mankind. When we shod our feet with the Gospel of peace, we stand in the truth of God's grace and mercy. We forgive as we have been forgiven. **We seek peace where previously we have run or tried to hide, pretend, or take control.** As far as it depends on us, we seek peace with God, self and others. We live a life of mercy and grace by seeking peace in our relationships, not harboring resentment and bitterness. *"Make every effort to live at peace...and see to it...that no bitter root grows up."* (Hebrews 12:14, 15 NIV)

*How does covering your feet with the Gospel of Peace help you?*

_____

_____

*How can you "shod your feet with the Gospel of peace" in your current struggle?*

_____

_____

_____

### 4. LIFT UP OVER ALL THE SHIELD OF FAITH

*"Lift up over all the (covering) shield of saving faith, upon which you can quench all the flaming missiles of the wicked (one)."* (Ephesians 6:16 AMP)

We have a tendency to live by what we see and hear, and trust our self-effort more than God's provision. But as God's children, we are to live by faith. Despite threats and fears, we resist our tendency to worry or take control. **We lean entirely on God in absolute trust and**

**confidence in Him alone to provide for and protect us**. In continuing our daily inventory, we look for what God will do in the midst of our circumstances.

We remember to *"be well balanced, be vigilant and cautious at all times; for that enemy of yours ... roams around like a lion roaring, seeking someone to seize upon and devour. Withstand him; be firm in faith (against his onset---rooted, established, strong, immovable, and determined)..."* (1Peter 5:8-9 AMP)

***Why is the Shield of Faith important for you, and how do you use it?***

_____

_____

***How can you lift up the Shield of Faith in your struggle today?***

_____

_____

## 5. TAKE THE HELMET OF SALVATION

*"And take the helmet of salvation..."* (Ephesians 6:17 AMP)

Our enemies will try to get us to forget who God is and who we are. But as a beloved child of God and a warrior in God's army, we pledge allegiance to Christ. *"You come from God and belong to God."* (1 John 4:6) **The Helmet of Salvation protects our minds, eyes, and ears from attacks of lies and deceptions when in battle.** When condemnation comes, **we remember that each of us is a child of God who is forgiven by the blood of Christ!** We do not let anyone or anything put us back into bondage or slavery to shame or guilt. We do not offer our allegiance to another.

***What does the Helmet of Salvation signify, and how does it help you?***

_____

_____

***How can you take the Helmet of Salvation in your current struggle?***

_____

_____

## 6. AND THE SWORD OF THE SPIRIT WHICH IS THE WORD OF GOD

*"And the sword that the Spirit wields, which is the Word of God..."* (Ephesians 6:17 AMP)

On our journey together, we learned the importance of God's truth to guide and teach us. But it is also an offensive and defensive weapon, probably the most important tool we will use in our daily inventory. We previously used blaming, lying, criticizing or justifying words as weapons to protect ourselves or overcome others. But **God's Word in our mind and mouth will separate truth from lies, and reveal His purposes.** *"So shall My Word be that goes* *forth out of My mouth; it shall not return to Me void (without producing any effect, useless), but it shall accomplish that which I please and purpose and it shall prosper in the thing for which I sent it."* (Isa 55:11 AMP) We can be successful in battle by knowing and speaking the Word of God with mercy and grace.

***How does the sword of the Spirit which is the Word of God help you?***

_____
_____

***How can you use the Sword of the Spirit to be successful in your current battle?***

_____
_____

### 7. PRAY IN THE SPIRIT

*"Pray at all times (on every occasion, in every season) in the Spirit, with all (manner of) prayer and entreaty. To that end keep alert and watch with strong purpose and perseverance, interceding in behalf of all the saints."* (Ephesians 6:18 AMP)

While we are weak, **we are not alone! God is with us! Our salvation includes receiving from God all the help we need. We stop holding God at a distance and ask for His help.** We keep our ears attentive to the voice of the Holy Spirit and pray to bring God into the battle with us. We pray at all times for courage and strength to persevere and overcome the attacks that come against us. We pray for others to persevere too, so that their hearts will be turned to God and they will receive the same healing and grace we have received. We pray for God's perspective and guidance and for His will to be done in all our decisions.

*"And this is the confidence (the assurance, the privilege of boldness) which we have in Him: (we are sure) that if we ask anything according to His will (in agreement with His own plan), He listens and hears us. And if we know that He listens to us in whatever we ask, we also know that we have (granted us as our present possessions) the requests made of Him."* (1 John 5:14-15 AMP)

***How do you see prayer as an essential part of your protective armor?***

_____
_____

***What can you pray--ask God for--in your current struggle?***

_____
_____

## **YOUR NEW LIFE**

You have now practiced Step 10 by putting on the full armor of God. In the midst of your present life circumstance, you have experienced the value of each piece of the armor God provided for you. Through the practice of a taking daily inventory and making amends when you are wrong, you improve your ability to stand firm in the face of pain and fear. You will grow stronger in your faith when you wear the full armor of God. Then as you wait and hope in God alone, you will see how He transforms your trials into blessings in the Land of Promise.

# STEPS INTO GOD'S GRACE

## LESSON 23: Be Rooted in God's Love

From the beginning of time, when He first envisioned our faces, God has been waiting for us to come into His arms. He yearned for us to know that only He could satisfy us. With tears in His eyes, He patiently waited to embrace us, hold us, and love us. But we, like Adam and Eve, chose to hide from Him in the fear and shame caused by our living outside the limits He set for us. While we sought so many other loves, He longed for us to come to know Him deeply, passionately, and intimately. Now that our time in the wilderness if finished, His hope is that we will not forget Him.

As we travelled into the wilderness, we learned that God is not a God who is far off, but a God who is near. His Holy Spirit went with us. He was present when we were faced with circumstances that tested our beliefs, exposed our deepest feelings and revealed our childish ways. We were humbled by the awareness of our dependence on ourselves and our false idols.

God wants us to remember how well He loved us. He held our hand, walked with us and talked with us. He whispered into our ears His words of love and truth, things too great for us to imagine. Out of His love, not anger, He showed us things we did not want to see, helped us overcome our fears, and healed our wounded hearts. He gave us companions to go with us. And as we travelled, we learned that no amount of money, beauty, possessions or success could bring us peace outside of God's love. We learned we no longer have to hide from Him and pretend we are someone else. We belong to God's family. We can hide in His love and live freely out of who He created us to be. His love is enough!

***What does God want you to remember from your journey with Him?***

_____

_____

The Holy Spirit reminds us, *"Your life is a journey you must travel with a deep consciousness of God."* (1 Peter 1:18 MSG) *"It's the well-trained who find themselves mature in their relationship with God!"* (Hebrews 12:11 MSG) *"Take diligent heed to... love the Lord your God and to walk in all His ways and to cling to and unite with Him and to serve Him with all your heart and soul (your very life)."* (Joshua 22:5 AMP) *"The object and purpose of your instruction and charge is love, which springs from a pure heart and a good (clear) conscience and sincere faith."* (1 Timothy 1:5 AMP)

***What kind of life are you to cultivate? How does your renewed mind and new heart prepare you for this life?***

_____

_____

# STEP 11: BE ROOTED IN GOD'S LOVE

*"Have the roots of your being firmly and deeply planted (in Him, fixed and founded in Him), being continually built up in Him, becoming increasingly more confirmed and established in the faith."* (Colossians 2:7 AMP)

Apart from God, our broken hearts could not offer or receive real love. We only reaped a crop of broken relationships filled with resentment and pain. But when we are rooted in God's love, we have the strength to love as God loves. Dale and Juanita Ryan describe the importance of this in *Rooted in God's Love.* (p. 14)

> "We all have root systems. Roots are life-lines. They seek out and drink in water and nutrients. And they provide stability in times of wind and erosion. Unfortunately, many of us are rooted in the soil of shame. Roots in this rocky soil become bound. They cannot sustain growth. They are not able to provide nourishment or stability. Recovery for many of us is like being transplanted. It is the process of allowing God to first **pull us out of the parched and rocky soil of shame and then plant us in the soil of love.** In the rich soil of love our fragile roots can finally begin to stretch, grow and take hold. It is a soil in which real nourishment and real stability are possible. But transplantation is not a simple matter…**As our roots sinks deeper and deeper in the soil of God's love, however, we will begin to experience growth that never could have been possible in the soil of rejection and shame. We will become "rooted and established" in love.**"

**Why is it important for you to be rooted in God's love?**
_____
_____

**What soils have your roots been in?**
_____

**How would you describe your ways of loving in the past, and what crop have you reaped?**
_____
_____

While I know God loves me and has done many great things for me, I can easily forget this when I face new struggles. I sometimes give my mind free reign to dwell on or obsess about my problems, or I allow busyness to keep me far from the stillness required to be present with God. If I am not careful, I forget what I have come to know as truth, sacrificing my freedom in Christ and returning to my old ways of taking control, hiding, covering and blaming!

*"Your fellowship with God enables you to gain a victory over the Evil One. Don't love the world's ways. Don't love the world's goods. Love of the world squeezes out love for the Father."* (1 John 2:15) *"I, God, am your Savior, your Redeemer, Champion...I give you only the best."* (Isaiah 60:16 MSG)

***What enables you to be victorious in this Life?*** _____

***How did you experience God's love towards you on this journey? What did He help you understand? How did He provide for your need?***
_____
_____
_____

***How does remembering what He did affect your ability to trust Him and love Him in this Life?***
_____
_____
_____

Unless we remember to cling to God every day, we will fall back into darkness and despair, that old miserable life. That is why we take **Step 11: *Sought through prayer and meditation to maintain conscious contact with God, praying only for the knowledge of His will for us and the power to carry it out.*** *"We live deeply and surely in him, and he lives in us. And this is how we experience his deep and abiding presence in us; by the Spirit he gave us."* (1 John 3: 24 MSG) *"Let us then approach the throne of grace with confidence, so that we may receive mercy and find grace to help us in our time of need."* (Hebrews 4:16 NIV)

***What do you need to do to help you in this new Life?***
_____
_____

***What will you experience when you take Step 11 in your new Life?***
_____
_____

1. **THROUGH PRAYER AND MEDITATION IMPROVE YOUR CONSCIOUS CONTACT WITH GOD**

   We no longer have to depend on our pitiful ways and limited understanding to make our way in this life. We are not alone. We can desperately cling to God for a renewal of our minds and a change of our hearts. We can be intentional to spend time with Him, to hear His voice and to depend on His Holy Spirit for guidance and wisdom. *"My sheep hear My voice, and I know them and they follow Me; and I give eternal life to them..."* (John 10:25-28 NASB) *"Listen to Me, listen well...pay attention, come close now, listen carefully to My life-giving, life-nourishing words."* (Isaiah 55:1-4 MSG)

I have learned that God's words to me are very specific for my circumstance. God does not reveal to me the whole journey, only the next step, and I will not hear any more from Him if I continually refuse to respond to what I have already heard. Seeking to know and hear God's voice can seem overwhelming, but after years of prayer to know God and hear Him, I am beginning to recognize His thoughts and will over my own. It has taken practice and diligence, but more often than not, when I least expect it or even want it, His thoughts come into my mind.

I firmly believe we all have the ability to have conversations with the Lord, and He knows exactly how to speak to us so we can hear. We must seek it and we will find it in His Word, by His Holy Spirit, or in a burning bush, or a dream or vision, or any other way He chooses to make His will known to us. *"He, who is able to hear, let him listen to and heed what the (Holy) Spirit says ..."* (Revelation 3:22 AMP)

***Do you believe you can hear God if you listen? Why?***
_____
_____

***Do you know Jesus' voice? Why?***
_____

***What changes are you willing to make in your new Life to help you improve your conscious contact with God?***
_____
_____

2. **PRAY TO KNOW GOD'S WILL**

Knowing God's will for us in any given moment is learned slowly. Despite the length of time I have been walking with Christ, I still often struggle to know where I am going and how I am going to get there. *"Steep your life in God reality, God initiative, God provisions. Don't worry about missing out. You'll find all your everyday human concerns will be met. Give your entire attention to what God is doing right now and don't get worked up about what may or may not happen tomorrow. God will help you deal with whatever hard things come up when the time comes...."* (Matthew 6:33-34 MSG)

***Give an example of a time you knew God's will for you.***
_____
_____

***What is one of the greatest obstacles to knowing God's will for <u>you</u>?***
_____
_____

*How can you give your entire attention to what God is doing right now in your life?*
_____
_____

### 3. HAVE GOD'S POWER TO CARRY OUT HIS WILL

In our old life, we relied on our limited power to make things work in our life. We medicated our pain and sought power through possessions, performance or other people. But we are not alone in the Land of Promise. God is with us! He will do for us what we cannot do for ourselves. When we choose to believe Him and are rooted in His love, we open ourselves to receive the power we need that only He can supply!

*"May He grant you out of the rich treasury of His glory to be strengthened and reinforced with mighty power in the inner man by the (Holy) Spirit. May you be rooted deep in love and founded securely on love, that you may have the power and be strong to apprehend and grasp with all the saints what is the breadth and length and height and depth (of it;). (Ephesians 3:16-18 AMP) Stop your silly efforts to save yourselves...Strength will come from settling down in complete dependence on Me (God)."* (Isaiah 30:15-17 MSG)

*What gives you power to carry out God's will?*
_____
_____

*What specific changes can you make in the Land of Promise to develop your conscious contact with God and become rooted in His love?*
_____
_____

## LIVE A LIFE OF LOVE

Only when we cling to God in this Life can we can fulfill our purpose to love as God loves.

*"I will show you a more excellent way (one that is better by far and the highest of them all – love)...Love endures long and is patient and kind; love never is envious or boils over with jealousy...is not conceited; it is not rude. Love (God's love in us) does not insist on its own rights or its own way, for it is not self-seeking; it is not touchy or fretful or resentful. Love bears up under anything. Love never fails."* (1 Corinthians 12:31-13:8 AMP)

*What kind of life are you to live?* _____

*What are characteristics of God's way of loving?*
_____
_____

Most of us are aware of how little our love resembled God's love. But now that we know we deeply loved by God, we are free to love as God loves in the Land of Promise. We will practice these new ways of loving while in relationship with others we encounter there. *"Just as I have loved you, so you too should love one another. By this all men shall know that you are my disciples, if you love one another."* (John 13:34-35 AMP)

***How will you learn how to love as God loves? Does this surprise you? Why?***

_____

_____

God's amazing love has healed and restored us! We have come out of the wilderness, leaning on our Beloved in desperate dependence for our life! We now know that for us to thrive in our new Life we must stay rooted in God's love. Even when all we hold dear is threatened, or pain is gripping our hearts, we must draw close to Him. We will refuse to fix or control problems, unless we are specifically directed by Him to do so. We will wait for His plan to unfold, confidently trusting in Him alone. He is our only hope!

***Why is Step 11, being rooted in God's love, so important to you in this Life?***

_____

***Believing this, what, will you do differently in this Life?***

_____

_____

*"This is my prayer: your love will flourish and that you will not only love much but well. Learn to love appropriately. You need to use your head and test your feelings so that your love is sincere and intelligent, not sentimental gush. Live a lover's life..."* (Philippians 1:9-10 MSG)

# STEPS INTO GOD'S GRACE

## LESSON 24: Love God

The Holy Spirit has led us to many places on our journey where we experienced the power of God's love to heal and transform us. While we have now been changed by His love, our journey is not over. We have been restored for a purpose: to be vessels of His love in the world! This does not mean we just talk about God's love in the Land of Promise. God desires us to respond to His love by loving Him in return!

*"My dear children, let us not just talk about love; let's practice real love. This is the only way we'll know we're living truly, living in God's reality."* (1 John 3:18-19 MSG) *"Chosen for this new life of love..."* (Colossians 3:12 MSG) *"Don't be lured away from him by the latest speculations about him. The grace of Christ is the only good ground for life".* (Hebrews 13:9 MSG) *"You shall love the Lord your God out of and with your whole heart and out of and with your soul (your life) and out of and with all your mind (your faculty of thought and your moral understanding) and out of, and with all your strength. This is the first and principal commandment."* (Mark 12:29-31 AMP)

***What kind of life have you been chosen for?*** _____

***Who are you to love most?*** _____

## REAL LOVE FOR GOD

When I first meditated on the charge to love the Lord with all my heart, mind and strength, I felt very anxious. While I thought I knew how to love my husband or my children, I was clueless about how to begin to love an invisible God. Even more, I was overwhelmed by the revelation that this is <u>the</u> most important purpose for my life.

***How do you feel knowing this is your primary purpose?***

_____

***Do you know how to love God with <u>all</u> your mind and your <u>whole</u> heart?*** _____

I realized I needed someone to show me how to practice real love toward my invisible heavenly Father. As I searched God's Word, I saw that Jesus faced this same dilemma. He showed me the way to live in the world, yet love my Father with an unending love.

1. Jesus acknowledged His identity as God's Son and recognized His Father's authority. (John 17:1; John 14:28; Luke 4:43).
2. He lived with a deep awareness of Truth and Reality. (John 8:14)
3. He loved His Father deeply and knew with certainty that His Father loved Him. (John 5:20; John 4:34)

4. He often spent time alone with His Father. (Luke 6:12)
5. He thought God's thoughts and lived by God's ways. (John 14:10; John 14:31; John 15:15; John 5:19)
6. He respected His Father's will and trusted His provision. (Matt 4:3-10)

*If you follow Jesus' lead, loving the Father as Jesus loved the Father, which of these practices will be most difficult for you? Why?*

___

## PRACTICE LOVING GOD WITH BOUNDARIES

**Most of our resentments are caused by the failure to love well.** If we want to live a life of peace, we must learn to love as God loves. For us to show our love and affection for God, as Jesus did, we respect God's established boundaries. We live mindful of what is ours to do and what falls under God's control. We respect God's authority and the free will of others. To love well, we maintain boundaries for our minds, hearts and actions.

Now let us consider various aspects of boundaries and how they influence our ability to love God:

1. ### RESPECT GOD'S BOUNDARIES OF IDENTITY

   a) Acknowledge God as God, your Father, Creator of all things, all-knowing, all-powerful, gracious, merciful and loving. His Kingdom has come and He has control and authority over all things.
   b) Acknowledge Christ as God's Son, your Savior and King, who has redeemed you.
   c) Acknowledge the Holy Spirit as Christ in you, your Comforter, Guide and Strength.
   d) Acknowledge that you are a unique child of God who is deeply loved and has a specific purpose in His Kingdom.

   You show your love for God when you acknowledge that you are His child and respect His authority. You are not consumed with establishing your own identity and kingdom, as others may be. You admit your unique limits and weaknesses and place your hope in God's power. **You are not in control, God is. Live confident in your Father's power, sovereignty, and goodness to provide for and protect you and your family.**

   *Consider how you feel when someone follows your direction or respects your authority. Does it stretch your imagination to think that God would feel the same way when you respect His authority? Can you see that respecting God's established order is a way of loving Him? Why?*

## 2. PUT BOUNDARIES AROUND YOUR MIND

a) Continually focus on God as the source of truth, not what you make up in your mind or learn from the world.
b) Do not trust your thinking or reasoning.
c) Allow the Holy Spirit and God's Word to teach you Truth.

You are a beloved child of God. Remember God's faithfulness and goodness. **Discipline your mind to think on Truth.** When you choose to meditate on and obey His Word, you show your desire to live within the boundaries of His Truth, not human reasoning. Keep your thoughts and beliefs focused on the present. Do not seek to figure out the future or control outcomes. That is not your concern; it belongs to God.

*Consider how you feel when someone trusts what you think or say. Do you think God might feel the same way when you trust Him? Can you see that filling your mind with God's truth is a way of loving God? Why?*

_____
_____

## 3. PUT BOUNDARIES AROUND YOUR HEART

a) Keep God as your first love.
b) Surrender your heart's desires and feelings, and align your will with God's will.
c) Ask God to remove the false idols and heal the broken, wounded places in your hearts.

Remember your Father loves you deeply. Do not let the selfish, sinful desires of the world become your desires. Shiny things and lures of pleasure cannot bring happiness. Remember God's love is never failing, and there is nothing you can do that will separate you from His love. **Keep Him as your first love and cling to Him for your very life.** Keep your heart open to Him. Do not let trials and suffering harden your heart or cause you to question God's love for you. When attacks of shame or guilt come against you, remember you are no longer under any condemnation. Do not run and hide as those in the world do. Bring your concerns and feelings to God.

*Consider how you feel when someone shares their deepest desires and feelings with you. Do you think God might feel the same way? Why might opening your heart to God be a way of loving Him?*

_____
_____

## 4. PUT BOUNDARIES AROUND YOUR ACTIONS

a) Wait for God's direction and provision. Remember you do not know what to do or when to do it. Live by faith.

b) Spend time with God and cling to Him in desperate dependence for your life!
c) Practice the Ways of examination, confession, repentance, forgiveness and peace.
d) Live with a ministry of reconciliation and love to bring God's Kingdom to the world.

You have been taught The Truth of your limitations and sin nature. You have been freed from your idols, healed of your wounds and personally taught the Ways of living by God. In your new life, there will be attempts to get you to rely on yourself and do things your way. Do not fall back into these old ways, but choose to live according to the ways of a child of God. Take responsibility to live what you say you believe.

***Consider how you feel when someone does what you advise them to do. Do you think God might feel the same way? Can you see how walking in God's ways is a way of loving Him? Why?***

_____

_____

God loves you and desires to be in intimate relationship with you. You show your love for Him when you spend time with Him. Busyness, distress, or your agenda will tempt you to keep God at a distance, but remember you no longer have to fear offending or disappointing Him. **Bring Him your hurts. Talk over your struggles. Be honest with Him. Seek to know Him.** Then wait and watch to see how He responds in your life!

***What busyness or distress tempts you to keep God at a distance? Why?***

_____

_____

***What boundaries can you set for your time together that would help you to share your life with Him?***

_____

_____

You will have to endure many trials in this new life. Sickness, death, or other losses will occur. When nothing makes sense, or everything you have is threatened or lost, trust God in the midst of the trouble. Even when you don't know 'why', hold fast to your faith. Remember to call to mind God's steadfast love for you, and hope in Him. Trust that He will show you the next step, and wait for Him to open a way. Rely on His provision and protection. Choose to believe and trust at all times. *"So if you find your life difficult ...take it in stride. Trust Him. He knows what He is doing, and He'll keep on doing it!"* (1 Peter 4:19 MSG)

*Consider how you feel when someone trusts you to help when they are helpless. Do you think God might feel the same way? Can you see that trusting God is a way of loving Him? Why?*

_____
_____

*What can you trust God with today to show Him your love?*

_____
_____

Finally, live with a ministry of reconciliation. Don't just talk about love, but practice real love. Your love for God is expressed by how well you love yourself and others in the Land of Promise.

*How can you express your love for God while in relationship with yourself and others in the Land of Promise?*

_____
_____

When my life was not the life I wanted, I resented God and depended on myself to get what I desired. I sought love in people, places or things. But now, with a deeper awareness of God's identity, my God-created identity, and God's love for me, I see my life in a new way. I know my trials have been allowed by God, and He will use them for good. My challenge is to love God in the midst of my trials by respecting and maintaining the boundaries He established for my good.

*What new understanding do you have about how to love God? How will this understanding change how you live in the Land of Promise?*

_____
_____
_____
_____

# STEPS INTO GOD'S GRACE

## LESSON 25: Love Yourself

Protected by God's armor and strengthened by His love, we can take the last step of our journey, **Step 12:** *Having had a spiritual experience as the result of these Steps, we tried to carry this message to others, and to practice these principles in all our affairs.* Practicing these principles includes loving ourselves and others, just as we are. *"You shall love your neighbor as you do yourself."* (Matthew 22:39)

Most of us never gave any consideration to God's direction in this commandment to love our neighbor <u>and</u> our self. As a result, we created our own identity and forced ourselves to live beyond <u>our</u> limits to achieve <u>our</u> heart's desires. We abandoned our self by minimizing our abilities and giftedness, or ignoring our feelings and weaknesses. As a result, we resented, or even hated, our less-than-perfect selves. We did not love ourselves.

But now we understand about boundaries. We have learned how to set boundaries to limit what we allow in our mind and heart. Now we will learn new actions we can take to love ourselves including both our weaknesses and strengths. But remember, we are still children who are just beginning to practice new ways of loving. We will fall down and make mistakes, but when we do, we will learn to offer ourselves the same mercy and grace God gives us. In the practice of Step 12, we will begin to love the beauty of our brokenness.

***In what ways have <u>you</u> failed to love yourself well?***
_____
_____

***How do you feel about the charge to love yourself? Why?***
_____
_____

## STEP 12: PRACTICE LOVING YOURSELF WITH BOUNDARIES

Many of us may have thought we were showing love to ourselves when we bought something new or took a vacation. While these actions may have made us happy, they were not healthy ways of loving ourselves. **Real love means we take responsibility for our identity as a child of God. We put boundaries around our mind and heart and the actions we take.**

***In the past, how did you practice loving yourself? What was the result?***
_____
_____
_____

*How are you to practice real love toward yourself?*

_____

_____

1. **RESPECT GOD'S BOUNDARY FOR YOUR IDENTITY**

   *"We're called children of God! That's who we really are."* (1 John 3:1 MSG) *"We're sticking to the limits of what God has set for us."* (2 Corinthians 10:13 MSG)

   You have allowed the world to define you, tell you what to wear, what to think, what to feel and what to do. Your identity was defined by who you married, the successes of your children, the job you held, or your achievements. The limits of your identity were the ones you chose for yourself, or the ones that were chosen for you by others. They were not the ones God established for you. But now you know the Truth of your God-given identity. *"Be content with who you are."* (1 Peter 5:6 MSG) **Love yourself by living within the limits of your God-given identity:**

   a) You are created by God, an image-bearer of God. You have intellectual, emotional, physical and spiritual needs and limits.
   b) You are a human being who is unique. You have God-given abilities/giftedness and purpose.
   c) You have a sin nature.
   d) You have been saved by Christ and have His Holy Spirit living in you.
   e) You are a citizen of the Kingdom of God and heir to God's promises.
   f) You are loved by God and He desires to transform you into the image of Christ.

   To love your God-created identity, you accept your weaknesses and celebrate your limitations. You stop any attempts to create a perfect image or discount your gifts. You don't to force yourself to be more or less than you are!

   ***Why is living within the limits of your God-given identity a way to love yourself?***

   _____

   _____

   For me, embracing my full God-given identity includes accepting my needs and valuing my unique abilities. This does not mean I lived entirely self-focused, but I do attempt to balance my needs with those of others. I do not compare my needs or abilities with those of others. I don't beat myself up for my lack of athletic prowess. I say "yes" to my needs for moderate amounts of rest, exercise, and time alone with God. I say "yes" to my needs for personal time, order and structure, one-on-one time with people and separate space. By acknowledging my needs as not less than or more important than those of others, I practice real love toward myself.

*What difference, if any, will your identity as a child of God make in how you live your new Life?*

_____
_____

**To answer the following questions, refer to list of Human Needs on the last page of this lesson.**

*What <u>general need</u> do you most struggle with fulfilling in a healthy way? Why?*

_____

*To help you meet that need, what could you say "yes" or "no" to?*

_____

*List the three <u>specific needs</u> that are most important to you.*

_____
_____
_____

*What could you say "yes" or "no" to, in order to better meet those needs?*

_____
_____
_____

2. **PUT BOUNDARIES AROUND YOUR MIND**

   At the Oasis of Examination God revealed the many lies you believed. You used your mind to create your own reality and deny your weaknesses, feelings and sin nature. You denied God's Truth and believed what the people in the world said. Then you lied to yourself to rationalize or justify your attempts to have life the way you wanted it. Now you have begun to fill your mind with truth. *"My dear children don't let anyone divert you from the truth."* (1 John 3:7 MSG) It is time to learn to put boundaries around your mind as a way of loving yourself:

   a) Choose to discern between Truth and illusion. Stop imagining a fairy tale life.
   b) Use your "yes" and "no" to choose what you let into your mind.
   c) Seek to live in the present, not the past or the future.
   d) Think loving, accepting, and forgiving thoughts about yourself.
   e) Set your mind on things that are true, noble, and pure—all the Truth in God's Word.
   f) Ask the Holy Spirit to guide you and help you control our thoughts.

   *Why is putting boundaries around your thoughts a way of loving yourself?*

   _____
   _____

I now know there is a difference between what seems right to me and what is actually true. I realize that I did not love myself well when I believed lies and ignored Reality. But now, because of the presence of the Holy Spirit, I can choose to see my life from God's perspective and fill my mind with Truth. To help myself stay grounded in Truth, I say "no" to romance novels which give me a skewed picture of real relationship. I say "yes" to God's Word, so I know Truth. I limit my exposure to newspapers, magazines and other media whose message is not consistent with God's Truth, because these may cause me to question or doubt God. Instead of thinking I have all the answers, I often say "I don't know," and pray for insight.

***What specific choices can you make to put boundaries around what you allow in your mind?***

_____

_____

3. **PUT BOUNDARIES AROUND YOUR HEART**

You were created for relationship; to receive and give real love. Consider loving yourself as God loves you. Delight in, listen to, value, accept and spend time with your God-created self. Take time to know your thoughts, feelings and deepest longings. Be available to yourself. Learn to be with yourself! Brenning Manning wrote in *Abba's Child* (p. 27):

> "To feel safe is to stop living in my head and sink down into my heart and feel liked and accepted...not having to hide anymore and distract myself with books, television, movies, ice cream, shallow conversation...staying in the present moment, not escaping into the past or projecting into the future, alert and attentive to the now...feeling relaxed and not nervous or jittery...no need to impress or dazzle others or draw attention to myself...Unself-conscious, a new way of being with myself, a new way of being in the world...calm, unafraid, no anxiety...loved and valued..."

***Why is spending time with you a way of loving yourself?***

_____

_____

***What might be some new ways you could practice "being with" yourself?***

_____

_____

You have spent many years without appropriate protection for your heart. You allow others' feelings to become your feelings and others' desires to become your desires. You give your heart to people who do not treat it with care. You carry others' sadness or pain as if it were your own, then blame God or yourself for the weight of it. You use your emotions to justify your actions. It is time to learn to put boundaries around your heart.

### a) BOUNDARIES FOR YOUR HEART: DESIRES
- Live with a deep awareness of your God-given mission to love.
- Seek to know and live out your specific purpose in building God's Kingdom.
- Do not allow the selfish desires of your sin nature to control your behaviors or keep you from loving and fulfilling your purpose
- *"Examine your desires and determine what is excessive, what is appropriate."* (1 Chronicles 11:15-19 MSG) *"Above all else, guard your heart, for it affects everything you do."* (Proverbs 4:23 NLT)

***Why are having boundaries around your desires a way of loving yourself?***
_____
_____

Stop living in conflict with the purpose for which you were created. Seek to know and live out God's purpose for you. You have been set free to love and build His Kingdom. Love yourself enough to embrace the reality of the mission you were given by God, and put boundaries around your heart to keep it pure and motivated by love.

***Why is learning to live out of your God-given desires a way of loving yourself?***
_____
_____

Each of us has desires given to us by God to motivate us to fulfill the purpose for which He created us. *"Each has his own special gift from God."* (1 Corinthians 7:7) This gift allows us to reflect some portion of God's love and facilitate the building of His Kingdom. To help you identify your God-given desire and purpose, review the following list:

1) Improve the world and make a difference
2) Help others
3) Motivate others to greater achievement
4) Know why and how things work
5) Fight for beliefs, community, or family
6) Boldly pursue life with an attitude of curiosity, adventure and optimism
7) Seek challenges and effect change
8) Pursue internal or external peace

***Which of the above most resonates with you as your God-given purpose? Why?***
_____
_____

When I was a small child, I followed others around and said, "I help, I help." I could not seem to stop myself from trying to meet every need. Today I understand it is just who I am; how God created me. To love myself well, however, I have to seek God's direction for me to know how and when to help. I cannot meet every need. Sometimes I have to say "no" to my selfish desires in order to to say "yes" to my God-given purpose. In different seasons of my life, I have had to say "no" to seeking significance in my work before I could say "yes" to care for my children, or later, to write and teach. I have learned that I feel most at peace when I am functioning in my God-given purpose, within the boundaries God sets for me.

*How can you live out your God-given purpose in your life today?*

_____
_____

*What can you say "yes" or "no" to which will facilitate living out your purpose at this moment?*

_____
_____
_____

### b) BOUNDARIES FOR YOUR HEART: FEELINGS
- Acknowledge and feel all your feelings, but do not act on all of them.
- Seek to keep a pure heart motivated by love, not fear, shame or guilt.

*Why is putting boundaries around your feelings a way of loving yourself?*

_____
_____

Many times in my life I felt agonizing pain from an unexpected hurt and shame from humiliating failure. I lashed out at God and condemned myself for not being enough to have prevented this suffering. But now I accept the reality that, because I was created to love, I have a heart that feels deeply. It can be easily hurt. Therefore, I love myself by guarding this precious part of my God-given identity. I do not deny my feelings; I acknowledge them to God and others. I seek to keep others' feelings separate from my feelings. I sit with my feelings. I do not run away from them or mindlessly react to them. I consider them to be warning lights that let me know there is something in my life that needs my attention.

*How can you put boundaries around your feelings?*

_____
_____

4. **PUT BOUNDARIES AROUND YOUR ACTIONS**

Much of your day will require you to care for children, work at a job, or complete other tasks. Look at everything in your life as an opportunity to practice real love toward others, but do not forget to love yourself as well. In the past, you ignored yourself, harshly judged your weaknesses, and condemned your failures. You punished and ridiculed yourself. You never learned how to be present with, listen to, or take care of your true self. You now know how selfish desires and hurt feelings can result in actions you regret. Love yourself by *"sticking to the limits of what God has set for you."* (2 Corinthians 10:13) Say "yes" to the right things and "no" to the wrong things.

   a) Abide in God's love and live God's way.
   b) Honor and respect yourself. Listen to and speak up for yourself.
   c) Have an attitude of mercy and grace towards yourself. Forgive yourself.
   d) Treat yourself with kindness. Speak to yourself with honest, gentle, and affirming words.
   e) Live one day at a time, not in the past or the future.
   f) Ask for help from others. Seek the guidance of the Holy Spirit.
   g) Function in your God-given abilities.

***Why is putting boundaries around your actions a way of loving yourself?***

_____

_____

Once I obtained a greater awareness of my physical needs, personal limits, sin nature, and unique purpose, I could make better choices to care for myself. I could protect myself from temptation and follow God's will for my life. Now I consider the quality and quantity of the food I eat, my need to rest, and appropriate amounts of exercise to keep me healthy. I have a high need for one-on-one time with others, so I take the initiative to be with friends, my children or husband. Since I am emotionally drained by spending excessive amounts of time with people or being in overly stressful situations, I intentionally spend time alone and limit the number of things I plan to do each day. I provide cushion between events in my day so I become less irritable when things take longer than I expect, which they often do. I don't always answer the phone when it rings. I don't say "yes" to every request or try to help with every need. I seek balance and moderation in my life. I seek to accept myself more and value my time, my needs and my life, as God does.

***What boundaries can you set around your actions to help you love yourself better?***

_____

_____

We may feel overwhelmed by all we are to do to love ourselves. But remember to *"trust God from the bottom of your heart; don't try to figure everything out on your own. Listen for God's voice in everything you do, everywhere you go; he's the one who will keep you on track. Don't assume that you know it all. Run to God!"* (Proverbs 3:5-6 MSG)

To live Life victoriously with a sin nature and human limits, we must stay connected to God. He is our safe place. We surrender our life of "trying harder" to embrace a life of "trusting God" throughout the day. We seek quiet places to talk with God and listen to His guidance. We read the Word and remember His faithfulness to us. We talk over all our problems with Him and seek to live by faith, not by sight. We become more comfortable with life's unknowns. We stop asking, "Why God?" We remember everything does not depend on us, and we look for what God will do in the midst of our circumstances.

***Why is choosing to trust God a way of loving yourself?***
_____

***What can you trust God with today in order to love yourself better?***
_____
_____

For much of my life I lived in resentment and fear, trying to force myself to be someone I was not. But now I am learning to accept my God-given identity, embrace my limits, and to regularly seek forgiveness for my harms. I use my "yes" and "no" more often to maintain my identity and limits. By maintaining boundaries with my choices, I love who God created me to be, and I try to live within the limits He sets for me.

***What have you learned about how to love yourself that has been most helpful for you?***
_____
_____

***How will the practice of loving yourself in Step 12 help you in your new Life?***
_____
_____

# HUMAN NEEDS

## General Needs (Needs of all humans)

1. Sleep
2. Food
3. Water
4. Exercise
5. Companionship with others
6. Connection with God

## Specific-Needs (Needs that vary in importance and necessity by person)

1. Personal Time
2. Need to give and do for others
3. Recognition for achievement
4. Approval and acceptance
5. Order and closure
6. Time alone
7. Financial security
8. Competition
9. Learning
10. Music
11. Have a project
12. Touch
13. Variety of experiences
14. Structured time
15. Unstructured time
16. One-on-one attention
17. Empathy
18. Humor

# STEPS INTO GOD'S GRACE

## LESSON 26: Love Others

Because our confidence in God's love for us is growing, we are beginning to love and accept ourselves as He does. Now we are ready to live out our purpose to love others in the Land of Promise. We can take the risk of opening our vulnerable hearts to others because what others think about us no longer determines our value or worth!

Once again we hear the voice of the Holy Spirit, "My dear children remember, *'God is love.'*" (1 John 4:16) "Love is the expression of God in you, a mature child of God. *Love your neighbor as (you do) yourself.*" (Matthew 22:39)

God wants us to know that this new Life is not about the job we hold or the accolades we achieve; it's about the people we love along the way. We have begun to learn how to love ourselves; now we will continue with Step 12 and learn to practice these principles toward others. Many of the people in the Land of Promise do not share our beliefs or values. These differences will provide opportunities for us to practice real love. We must remember to **love with boundaries for our mind, heart and actions.**

*What are you called to do with others in the Land of Promise? Why?*

_____

_____

*How do you feel about this charge?*

_____

## STEP 12: PRACTICE LOVING OTHERS WITH BOUNDARIES

Relationships are God's gift to you; a place for you to grow in your capacity to love as Christ loved. God has placed you in a family, church or job that is a fertile field for you to mature in your ability to love in the midst of brokenness and differences. Relationships are not vehicles for you to assert your power and control or to get your needs met on your terms. Relationships provide opportunities to offer love that understands, accepts, and encourages others to grow into who God created them to be. It is time to practice new ways of living in community.

*What is God's purpose for relationships and how does this compare to what you thought relationships were for?*

_____

_____

When I did my inventory, I learned that I struggled in my past relationships because I failed to love well. I was threatened by others' intelligence or accomplishments and dependent on their approval in order to believe that I mattered. My love was selfish and self-centered. But now that I am confident in God's love for me, I can love more freely, without needing anything in return. I love as God loves when I respect who God is and who I am, and live the way He has called me to live.

*"The whole world is under the power of the evil one. And you know that the Son of God has come to this world and has given you understanding and insight...Little children, keep yourselves from idols (false gods)--from anything and everything that would occupy the place in your heart due to God."* (1 John 5:19-21 AMP)

1. **RESPECT THE BOUNDARIES OF HUMAN IDENTITY**

    We are all different, yet each created by God. It is all part of His perfect and divine plan. When we remember we are unique, limited humans, we can let go of unrealistic expectations of perfection for others. We can accept others as they are. We can respect the limits and differences of each human, not compare or judge them. We remember that we each have a sin nature which can cause us to react out of fear, be controlled by shame and guilt and seek satisfaction of our needs in people or things. We will disagree. Others will try to have their own way. But God's forgiveness toward us allows us to offer forgiveness to others. Our challenge in the Land of Promise is to love others while not allowing them to affect our identity as a child of God.

    When I stopped and looked at the people around me, I saw very busy people rushing to do the next thing. With their faces down, they were more connected to their phones than the people around them. I heard angry, condemning words from people who seemed to think they knew best or resented interruptions to their agenda. I saw hands that punished and feet that ran away. They seemed to have no time or desire to know me or God.

    ***How would you describe the people you see in the Land of Promise?***
    _____
    _____

    ***How would you describe a person in your family that is difficult for you to love?***
    _____
    _____

    But when I look at them with the eyes of my heart, I see frightened children, dressed like adults, who are blind to the Truth. I see their wounded hearts and their struggles with shame, fear and guilt. I recognize their attempts to ignore their limits and deny their uniqueness in order to be like others, in order to feel a sense of belonging. I realize they are people like me who are in need of the healing hand of God.

*Describe the same person in your family with the eyes of your heart.*
_____
_____

*How does this affect your ability to love them as God loves you? Why?*
_____
_____

*Consider a current relationship. How does remembering <u>their</u> true identity as a God-created, unique, limited human with a sin nature help you love them better?*
_____
_____

*How does this person challenge your ability to live within <u>your</u> identity as a unique, limited child of God with a sin nature?*
_____
_____

The greatest challenge will be to maintain our identity when in relationship with others. When we were dependent on others' approval for our significance or belonging, we often made their beliefs, desires or actions our own. But now, because of God's love for us, we do not need others' love. Because of our trust in God, we do not have to fear being swallowed up by their need or frightened by their differences. Everything does not depend on us. We can set boundaries around our mind, heart and actions, and love them unconditionally.

2. **<u>PUT BOUNDARIES AROUND YOUR MIND</u>**

Fellowship with others is a blessing from God, but it can provide the greatest tests to your ability to remain grounded in the Truth. As you love others, **do to not let their beliefs become your beliefs.**

I am often reminded that I tend to make assumptions about what others say or do. I tend to make up reasons for their behavior and assign meanings to their actions without knowing facts. Only because of God's grace toward me in the wilderness am I aware of the lies I have believed. He has taught me how to renew my mind with Truth. But I must live with many of people who have not yet come to know the same Truth. They still believe that others are responsible for their happiness, they are responsible for others' happiness, or they know what is best for others. My challenge is to not to let others' beliefs become my beliefs, but to intentionally stop and test everything I see and hear against God's truth while I seek to love them as they are.

*How is your mind tested in your relationships with others?*

_____
_____

*Consider a current relationship. Give an example of how you put boundaries around your mind to help you stay in the Truth.*

_____
_____

3. **PUT BOUNDARIES AROUND YOUR HEART**

Real love of real people is not dependent on performance, job, heritage, or accomplishments. Real love is a heart connection with each other's humanity. It develops over time as you experience joy and pain together. It can be messy because of your differences and sin natures. Guard your heart. Test the feelings and motivations of your heart against God's truth to see if you are in fear or love, control or faith, self-seeking or peace-keeping. Approach others with a pure heart, then share your needs and desires and seek to know theirs. Remember to **respect the separateness between your feelings and desires and those of another**.

When you separate your feelings and desires from those of others, you can hear another's pain and sadness with a heart of compassion, without making it about you or allowing their feelings to debilitate you. Practice detaching from any shame or guilt others may use to condemn or control you by reminding yourself of your redemption and forgiveness through Christ. When you are grounded in God's love and the truth that He is in control, you are less likely to be overwhelmed or threatened by the feelings and desires of others, or the need to take control to fix them.

*How is your heart tested when in relationship with others?*

_____
_____

*Consider a current relationship. Give an example of how you put boundaries around your heart to help you love them and yourself well.*

_____
_____
_____

4. **PUT BOUNDARIES AROUND YOUR ACTIONS**

You will want to tell others how to live and what is true. That is God's job, not yours. Others need to take their own journey before God, on whatever path they choose. Your job is not to disrupt the path they choose but love them along the way. Love them enough to tell them the Truth. Speak to them kindly and do for them only as directed by God. But do not attempt to do for them what they need to learn to do for themselves. This only weakens them. It does not build them up. Trust God with their lives. Bring the same love Jesus brought into the world: a love that knows brokenness but loves anyway. This kind of love will require long-suffering. You will feel pain and sadness because you love, but you will also have the opportunity to share joy. This is abundant life. Remember to stay connected to God as you love yourself and others.

*"The whole point of what we're urging is simply love – love uncontaminated by self-interest and counterfeit faith, a life open to God...It's true that moral guidance and counsel need to be given, but the way you say it and to whom you say it are as important as what you say."* (1 Timothy 1:5, 8)

Love others, one person at a time. Be present and available. Be intentional to spend time with them. Get to know them and allow them to know you. Be the one who listens with your heart to their deepest longings, struggles and dreams without judgment. Speak the Truth in love.

Sometimes your time together will be devoted to accomplishing tasks or having fun. But loving well means taking time to build intimacy too. To do this, pause, look at each other, and listen not just with your ears, but with your heart. The depth of what you share will depend on the nature of the relationship and how safe you feel with that person. But if you feel safe, share not just the facts of your everyday lives, but what breaks your heart, brings you to tears, or makes you smile. How much time you spend with someone will be dependent on your emotional or physical limits. You can be intentional to maintain a balance in the time you spend with others, yourself and God. Learn how to listen and respect the thoughts, feelings and limits of others without trying to change them or allowing them to change you.

**Think of someone you love. How can you spend time with them while at the same time respecting your limits?**

_____

_____

I now know that healthy boundaries define where I end and another person begins. When I have healthy boundaries, I am mindful of my limits and respectful of the limits of others. I listen with a desire to know others. While I show sympathy for others, I do not try to fix or rescue them. I offer words of encouragement, expressing my belief that they know what is best and will make the right decision. I contain my desire to do something for them that they need to learn to do for themselves. Unless directed otherwise by God, I say "no" when I am not willing to do something that exceeds my limits or is outside of my value system. I accept a "no" from someone else, without trying to change them. I respect the identity and responsibilities of others by giving them the dignity of experiencing the consequences of their choices. I practice giving them the freedom to make mistakes and take responsibility for their life before God. I do not interfere, rescue or enable them. When I wrong another, I humbly confess my wrong and seek forgiveness. I offer the same forgiveness to others for their wrongs. I practice trusting God with their lives, not demanding my way for them. I practiced the Ways of God.

*These ways of loving will be new to you. To help you learn how to love others as God loves, review the worksheet:* **LOVE OTHERS IN HEALTHY WAYS** *at the end of the lesson and then answer the following questions.*

*Consider a current relationship. How can you listen, speak and act differently to practice real love toward them?*

_____
_____
_____

*In what relationship do you think you need to set a limit by saying "no"? How can you say "no"?*

_____
_____
_____

*Did someone tell you "no" recently? Were you able to respect that "no"? Why?*

_____
_____

I wanted a formula to follow to help me love others. But God showed me that trying to follow a formula was my way of still trying to stay in control and depend on myself. God's way is not based on a formula but on a relationship with Him. Only through a moment by moment dependence on God and His Holy Spirit could I know the truth and walk in it. He is my only source of hope and help. I can only carry out my purpose to love God, self and others in a broken world by desperate dependence on God! He will reveal the truth and help me know what to do or say. He is the only one in control of outcomes. Trusting God means I trust His timing, provision, protection and ways, despite what I think or feel. Others are not responsible to fix me, and I do not have the responsibility to fix another. That is God's responsibility. I choose to **live what I say I believe. I am a limited human-being living in a limited world with an unlimited God who will do for me and others what we cannot do for ourselves!**

*How does trusting God help you love others?*

_____
_____

*"If there are corrections to be made or manners to be learned, God can handle that without your help....each person is free to follow the convictions of conscience....None of us are permitted to insist on our own way...It's God we are answerable to---all the way from life to death and everything in between---not each other...So where does that leave you when you criticize a brother? And where does that leave you when you condescend to a sister? I'd say it leaves you looking pretty silly---or worse...so tend to your own knitting. You've got your hands full just taking care of your own life before God. Forget about deciding what's right for each other."* (Romans 14:4-13 MSG)

***Who do you need entrust to God?*** _____

***What is your responsibility in another's life? In your life?***
_____
_____

## **CONFLICTS WILL ARISE**

Our relationships with others can be beautiful, but they can also be dangerous. Conflicts will arise. Feelings will be hurt and negotiation will be required. Living in the Land of Promise means we accept that there will not always be peace in our relationships, but conflict can be a stepping stone to better relationships and spiritual growth.

Conflicts in relationships provide opportunities for us to practice loving people who are different from us. Conflicts challenge us to release the choke hold we had on others when we demanded, expected, or needed others to be who we thought they should be. Conflicts help us practice acknowledging and calming our feelings so that we communicate kindly and with respect. Conflicts help us learn to practice healthy ways of speaking, listening, forgiving, and negotiating.

***Why will conflicts arise? How can you practice loving yourself and another during conflict?***
_____
_____
_____

I have learned several helpful guidelines for my behavior when conflict arises. I do not confuse the present matter with the past. I stay in the present and speak honestly, using "I statements" that are kind and direct. I speak the truth in love, which means I am vulnerably honest. I reveal my true thoughts and feelings. I no longer seek to impress or control, but to communicate honestly even when I feel afraid, sad or angry. I seek peace through communication and love.

*"So let's agree to use all our energy in getting along with each other. Help others with encouraging words; don't drag them down by finding fault...Cultivate your own relationship with God, but don't impose it on others. You're fortunate if your behavior and your belief are coherent. But if you're not sure, if you notice that you are acting in ways inconsistent with what*

*you believe---some days trying to impose your opinions on others, other days just trying to please them,---then you know that you're out of line. If the way you live isn't consistent with what you believe, then it's wrong."* (Romans 14:19-23 MSG)

**<u>Refer to the LOVE OTHERS IN CONFLICT worksheet at the end of the lesson</u>. Using this format, write out a conversation to help you confront a current conflict.**

_____
_____
_____
_____

Without a clear understanding of God's love for me and His desire to provide for me, I used human relationships to try to satisfy my needs. I depended on others' approval to gain significance. Out of fear of rejection, I hid my limits and weaknesses, or failed to communicate my wants and needs. I seldom said no and pretended to like the same things to get along. I expected others to take care of me, and I believed that I was expected to take care of them. My ways of loving did not build up others; it enabled them. But now as I am growing in my capacity to love God, self and others in the midst of differences and conflict, I am thankful for all my relationships, even those that are painful.

My Life in the Land of Promise includes conflict and pain. It includes times when I must fight against overwhelming odds to keep my heart open, even though I may be rejected. It is a life that includes making hard choices, like choosing to stay in a relationship when my desire to quit is strong. It is a life where, in the midst of suffering, I choose to love, because it really is all I have to offer another. It is a life of promise because I can trust God to do for me what I cannot do for myself while I live the life He wants me to enjoy!

**What practical boundaries have you learned that will help you love others in your new Life?**

_____
_____
_____
_____

# LOVE OTHERS IN HEALTHY WAYS

## LISTEN WITH THE EYES OF YOUR HEART

- Listen with complete focused attention. Put away your cell phone, stop thinking about something else, and stop doing more than one thing at a time.
- Listen to know and understand the other person's identity and values, not to formulate a defense.
- Listen without interruption, judgment, condemnation or ridicule.
- Respect the other person as someone worthy to get to know.
- Do not assume all you hear is about you.
- Do not assume you already know what they are going to say or what they mean.

## PAUSE

- Consider whether you can respond in a healthy way, or if you need take time to process what you just heard to allow your emotions time to calm down.
- If you need some time, ask for it, and let the other person know when you will be able to respond. For example: "Let me think about that. I'll get back with you tomorrow."

## SPEAK THE TRUTH IN LOVE

- Be honest when you respond. Use words that reveal your true beliefs, feelings and desires.
- Have a humble attitude. Use words that are non-judgmental, kind and gentle.
- Say "yes" when you mean "yes" and "no" when you mean "no."
- Do not shrink to a child who resorts to crying and whining, or grow into a giant who seeks to control and dominate. Be willing to negotiate.
- Give encouragement as often as possible, advice only when asked and judgment never. Do not take pride in having answers, but speak only what and when guided by the Spirit.

(Healthy speaking does not include yelling or screaming, criticism or ridiculing, sarcasm, lying, interrupting, blaming, fixing, or monopolizing a conversation)

## ACT WITH MERCY AND GRACE

- Love is kind and respectful. Ask permission to stand in someone's personal space, touch them or their belongings.
- Keep commitments when possible. Love never gives up.
- Do not allow verbal or physical abuse. Walk away when necessary.
- Trust God, live by faith, and seek peace.
- Pursue your own life before God and give others the freedom to pursue theirs. Do not demand your own way in the lives of others.
- Keep no record of wrongs. Confess, ask for and offer forgiveness often.

# LOVE OTHERS IN CONFLICT

1. **Kindly and respectfully repeat what the person said or did.**

    *"When I heard you say ....or saw you do..."*

2. **Honestly state <u>your</u> perception, assumptions, interpretation, imagining, or thoughts about what was said or done.**

    *"What I made up about that is....."*

3. **Share <u>your</u> emotions--anger, fear, pain, joy, passion, love, guilt, shame.**

    *"And about that I feel..."*

4. **Ask for what you want, but let go of any expectations.**

    *"Would you be willing to ...?"*

5. **If necessary, establish consequences or negotiate options.**

    *"If you continue to ......I will...."*

6. **Let go of the outcome, trust God and pray.**

# STEPS INTO GOD'S GRACE

## LESSON 27: Your Life is the Message of God's Love

It has been a long and difficult journey. Together we have travelled to the highest mountains and the lowest valleys as we followed the Holy Road our Father opened before us. We have been supernaturally transformed by His love. We no longer have to live in the darkness of the world, controlled by our sin nature. We no longer have to rely on our own efforts to make life work and to prove we are loved. Because of God's love and Christ's resurrection, we are free to live an abundant life in the Land of Promise. Leaning on our Beloved in desperate dependence, we can live the Life He wants us to enjoy!

The quiet voice we have learned to know so well now comes with our final instructions:

"My little children, remember you were once separated from God and dead in your transgressions and sin. But by God's grace, you were chosen, adopted as His sons and daughters and restored to relationship with Him. Do not forget your time in the wilderness where God worked to lovingly and carefully restore you to your true identity and inheritance. You were personally taught the mysteries and secrets of God's Kingdom. You were blind but now you see. You experienced the miraculous power of God's ways of examination, confession, repentance and forgiveness to free you from your bondage to shame, guilt and fear. You experienced the healing, transforming power of God, which delivered your hearts from idols so you could love as God loves. You are now His sons and daughters living in the Land of Promise. Temptations and trials will come. When your identity and safety are challenged, practice what you have learned. Stay close to Me. I will show you the way. Remember Christ is with you always. You are not just fighting only for your own minds and hearts, but also for the minds and hearts of all God's children. Remember to put on the armor of God to fight the battles as you go forward to love God, self and others."

*"You are a letter of Christ... not written with ink, but with the Spirit of the living God; not on tablets of stone but in tablets of human hearts...your power and ability and sufficiency are from God ... (making us to be fit and worthy and sufficient) as ministers and dispensers of a new covenant, not of the letter but of the Spirit; for the code kills, but the Spirit makes alive....* (2 Corinthians 3:3-6 AMP) *You are the ones chosen by God, chosen for the high calling of priestly work, chosen to be a holy people, God's instruments to do His work and speak out for Him, to tell others of the night-and-day difference He made for you---from nothing to something, from rejected to accepted."* (1 Peter 2:8-10 MSG)

*"It is clear ...that God not only loves you very much but also has put his hand on you for something special. ...the news of your faith in God is out...**you're the message!** Just quietly present your healed body...along with the appropriate expressions of thanks to God. Your cleansed and grateful life, not your words will bear witness to what I have done.* (Matthew 8:4 MSG) *You are my witnesses...you're my handpicked servant so that you'll come to know and*

*trust me, understand both that I am and who I am...I am God...the only Savior there is. ...**You're my witnesses, you're the evidence.*** " (Isaiah 43: 10- 13 MSG)

**Do you believe God has put His hand on you for something special? What?**

_____

_____

## MY MESSAGE

As I came to understand and believe that God had chosen me and healed me, I felt overwhelmed by His charge to bear witness to what He had done. I was uncomfortable with the confidence God was placing in me to be one of His handpicked servants who would come to know Him and speak out for Him. Slowly, however, the Holy Spirit settled my fears and reminded me I was not alone. I had the presence of Christ in me, God's Word, and the strength of my companions to hold me up. Now, many years after hearing these words for the first time, I cautiously live more mindful of my true identity as a beloved Child of God who is called to be a witness of who God is and what He has done in my life.

My life is not perfect. I am not perfect. I spent the first 40 years of my life living my way. I sought power and significance in my performance. I sought security in others' approval or love for me. But after reaping a crop of broken relationships, a failed marriage and disgrace, I was willing to surrender to God. Over the next 20 years, God faithfully, but very slowly, guided me and worked in me. I never knew what lay ahead, and I was often afraid. But He held my hand tightly and walked with me through many very dark places.

Throughout my journey, God revealed the idols of my heart: my children, other people, my image, job, and financial security. I depended on these idols to make my life work, instead of depending on God. He showed me how I used people to get my needs met and how I valued the opinion of others more than His. As He removed my idols, I often wailed and fell back into self-pity, but I learned He was the only one I could really trust and depend on to care for me and keep me safe.

God exposed my wrong belief that everything depended on me. When I let go of this lie, He helped me learn that He was my only hope. He showed me the foolishness of depending on myself, my possessions or other people's opinions to make me feel secure and safe. Sometimes the pain was so great I thought I would die. Often I tried to run away and hide. But I now know that God uses pain to teach me about myself or Him. In the midst of pain, He helps me face and overcome my fears of rejection and making mistakes. Through my struggles in marriage and as a parent, He teaches me about my selfish love and helps me practice His ways of loving. Replacing my wrong beliefs with His Truth, my shame and guilt with His love, and my pitiful ways of living with His Ways, I have slowly begun to live in reality. I have begun to accept the world as it is, not as I would have it: a world where God is in control of all things, and I am not.

I can now attest to the Truth that God miraculously raised me from my dead life of self-effort, shame and condemnation, to give me a new life as His child. He continually gives me grace and mercy for my sins and failures, provides the love and care I desperately need, and He graciously teaches me how to live in His Kingdom of Grace.

I expect that my journey will always include failure and success, and joy and pain, as God continues to transform me and grow me up into the image of Christ. I am becoming more willing to submit to these changes with each new experience of God's goodness and faithfulness in my life. God is not done with me. He continues His work to transform me into the image of Christ. I still make mistakes. I sometimes struggle to accept His will over my own. I resist giving up my ways to practice His Ways. I even forget that He is always with me and will not forsake me. Sometimes I doubt or fall into fear. But I am thankful that the Holy Spirit continues to remind me of the Truth and gives me other companions to help me stay strong because I want to be faithful to God's purpose for my life which is: *"Go, take your stand in the temple courts and declare to the people the whole doctrine concerning this Life."* (Acts 5:20)

My Message is this: I know Jesus lives! He is alive in me! I believe this because the same power that conquered His grave has raised me up to new life. I was blind and deaf to the truth, but because of His grace, now I see and hear! I was lame when I tried to live by my self-effort, but now because of God's grace, I stand strong in His love and have the presence of the Holy Spirit in me! Now I know and proclaim, "It is all God's grace". It is not by my might, but by God's grace and His Holy Spirit that I am continually restored to new life.

*"Not by might, nor by power, but by My Spirit says the Lord of hosts. ... He shall bring forth the finishing gable stone (of the new temple) with loud shoutings of the people, crying Grace, grace to it!"* (Zechariah 4:6-7 AMP)

## **YOUR LIFE IS THE MESSAGE OF GOD'S LOVE**

Resolve today that you are chosen, beloved and blessed by God. Now go, be a blessing to His other Children who find themselves in difficult times and are looking for someone to help them know what is true and how to continue to live in times of affliction. Remember, however, your responsibility or purpose is **not** to save the world! Christ has already done all that is necessary to accomplish that. You are only to allow the light of what Christ has done in you to shine in the Land of Promise. You were once blind, deaf, and lame, but you have experienced the healing power of Christ in your life! Your changed life is God's message of His grace!

You are to continually practice **Step 12:** *Having had a spiritual experience as the result of these Steps, we tried to carry this message to others, and to practice these principles in all our affairs.* Live out of your unique God-given identity and purpose. Love graciously and generously as God loves you. Be a companion to those who live in prisons of shame, guilt, resentment and fear. Encourage them during their dark times. You can offer hope and compassion because you experienced many of the same challenges and tribulations they are facing. Through painful times you came to know God's faithfulness and experienced His power in your life. Tell others about your past wounds, blind eyes and slavery to false idols. Speak of God's grace toward you through His mighty blessings of truth, freedom, healing and restoration to new life. Speak of the resurrection life that God gave you and His desire to rescue and redeem them too. Encourage others to let go of their self-dependence to trust in the unfailing love and power of God. Encourage them to seek His face, voice, and presence continually; because you now know that this is the only place to find hope and peace. Help them know the Truth and the Way, and offer them hope by witnessing of your experience of the saving and redeeming grace of God. Then set them free to walk their own journey with God.

Live mindful of your identity as a Child of God. But also remember you are a limited, unique human with a sin nature who still has much to learn. You will at times struggle with fear, selfishness and self-centeredness on your journey ahead. You will face more trials and difficulties. Remember it is only by God's power and strength that you can overcome. Stand rooted and grounded in God's love. Do not forget the steps into God's grace. Continually practice examination, confession, repentance and forgiveness. Most of all, lean on God in desperate dependence. Live one day at a time, waiting, listening, trusting, moving, and resting only as God directs.

*"We declare what we have heard, what we have seen with our own eyes, what we have looked at and touched with our hands, concerning the word of life. This Life was revealed and we have seen it and testify to it and declare ...the eternal life that was with the Father and was revealed to us. We declare to you what we have seen and heard so that you also may have fellowship with us; and truly our fellowship is with the Father and with His Son Jesus Christ....that our joy may be complete."* (1 John 1:1-4 NRSV)

## **WRITE YOUR MESSAGE**

Now it is time for you to reflect on each step of your journey into God's grace--to record what you heard, saw and experienced of God's supernatural power for you as His child. Your changed life is the unique message of God's grace. You are the evidence that the Kingdom of God exists and Jesus is alive and reigning as King!

I pray that you will remember to live with a deep awareness of God's grace toward you and His purpose for your life. Be strengthened by God's love for you. Know and fight for the Truth. Love without expectation. Offer mercy and grace toward others. Desperately depend on Christ alone. Your life is the Message of the Truth, the Way and the Life for all God's children in the world!

*"Salvation and power are established! Kingdom of our God, authority of his Messiah! The Accuser of our brothers and sisters thrown out, who accused them day and night before God. They defeated him through the blood of the Lamb and the bold word of their witness."* (Revelation 12:10-11 MSG)

**Your message is your personal experience with Jesus. He chose you, restored your sight, taught you the Truth, released you from captivity to idols and deception, and delivered you from the power of sin, shame, guilt, and fear. This word of your testimony will help others come into the light of the Truth, the Way and the Life God desires for all His children!**

*As the final exercise of this study, complete the questions on the following pages and write Your Message. Then share Your Message with at least one person who was not on the journey with you, and be prepared to share Your Message with your travelling companions at the next meeting.*

# WRITE YOUR MESSAGE

Go back over your prior lessons and reflect on your journey. Consider how the whole gospel of Jesus Christ and the power and presence of the Holy Spirit have radically transformed your beliefs, feelings, ways, identity and purpose. Answer the following questions to help you write Your Message. Then, using a separate sheet of paper, write about your spiritual experience with God on this journey. Though this may just seem like a summary of what you have already learned, it is critical to complete the following questions to record all you have experienced on this journey so that you can write Your Message.

1. *What was your life like when you first began this journey?* Describe what you were struggling with, what you were feeling powerless over, or what was causing you pain or fear. Why were you seeking hope or peace?

   _____
   _____
   _____

2. *How difficult was it for you to surrender as king of your kingdom? Why?*

   _____
   _____

3. *What Truth did you hear at the Oasis of Examination?* How you were blind or deaf to the Truth? How did your sin nature manifest itself in your life? (Possibilities to consider: lies believed or hardened or frozen feelings of your heart)

   _____
   _____
   _____
   _____

4. *What wrong beliefs, sinful desires or harmful actions did you confess at the Mountain of Confession?* What did you depend on for your identity, safety or love instead of God?

   _____
   _____
   _____

5. *What wrong belief, sinful desire or harmful behavior did God help you let go of at the Valley of Repentance?*

   _____
   _____
   _____

6. *What did God do to raise you to new life at the Pool of Transformation? What lie did God remove from your mind? What bondage or fear in your heart did God deliver you from? What thoughts or desires did God cleanse from your mind or heart?*

   _____
   _____
   _____

7. *What forgiveness did you receive or offer at the River of Forgiveness or on the Pathway of Peace?* What healing did you experience?

   _____
   _____
   _____

8. *What new ways of living were you taught that were most helpful to you?*

   _____
   _____
   _____

9. *What is the Truth you now know about your God-given identity and purpose? What have you come to know about God's character?*

   _____
   _____
   _____

10. *Has your trust in God changed since you started the journey? Why?* What was your personal experience of God's power, character, faithfulness and love? How has that affected your ability to trust Him?

    _____
    _____
    _____

11. *Describe how your life is different now from when you began your journey.* What hope can you offer to another in their time of struggle because of your spiritual experience with God? What does your cleansed and freed life bear witness to?

    _____
    _____
    _____

*Now write Your Message using your answers to these questions as a guide.*

## Epilogue

I have tried my best to be faithful to tell each of you the whole truth about this life. I pray that you now know more of how much God loves you. I pray you know you are not, and have never been alone. God has been with you every step of the way, and He will be with you with every new step you take. As His beloved child, may you trust in His love, depend on His faithfulness, and continue to enjoy His amazing grace, each and every day!

# Steps into God's Grace

## The Twelve Steps

1. We admitted we were powerless sin and that our lives are unmanageable.

2. We came to believe that a power greater than ourselves could restore us to sanity.

3. Made a decision to turn my life and my will over to the care of God.

4. Made a searching and fearless moral inventory of ourselves.

5. Admit to God, to ourselves, and to another human being the exact nature of our wrongs.

6. Were entirely ready to have God remove all these defects of character.

7. Humbly asked God to remove our shortcomings.

8. Made a list of all persons we had harmed and became willing to make amends to them all.

9. Made direct amends to such people wherever possible, except when to do so would injure them or others.

10. Continued to take personal inventory and, when we were wrong, promptly admitted it.

11. Sought through prayer and meditation to improve our conscious contact with God, praying only for knowledge of His will for us and the power to carry that out.

12. Having had a spiritual awakening as the result of these steps, we tried to carry this message to others, and to practice these principles in all our affairs.

# Steps into God's Grace

## Optional Reading

### Recovery Resources

Beattie, Melody *Codependents' Guide to the Twelve Steps*. New York: Simon & Shuster, 1998.

May, Dr. Gerald G. *Addiction and Grace*. New York: HarperOne, 2007.

Miller, J. Keith *A Hunger for Healing*. New York: HarperOne, 1992.

### Spiritual Growth

Benner, David G. *Surrender to Love*. Downers Grove: IVP Books, 2003.

Cloud, Dr. Henry and Townsend, Dr. John *Boundaries*. Grand Rapids: Zondervan, 1992.

Fenelon, *Let Go*. New Kensington: Whitaker House, 1973

Foster, Richard J. *Life with God*. New York: Harper One, 2008.

Meyer, Joyce *Battlefield of the Mind*. New York: Warner Faith, 2002.

Peterson, Eugene *The Message: The Bible in Contemporary Language*. Colorado Springs: NavPress, 2005.

Willard, Dallas *Divine Conspiracy*. New York: Harper Collins, 1998.

### Devotionals

Beattie, Melody *Language of Letting Go*. Center City: Hazelden, 1990

Roberts, Frances J. *Come Away, My Beloved*. Uhrichville: Barbour, 1973

Young, Sarah *Jesus Calling*. Nashville: Thomas Nelson, 2004.

Printed in Great Britain
by Amazon.co.uk, Ltd.,
Marston Gate.